# Model Railway Constructor

...AN

**SPECIAL**

# 7. Model Drawings Reference Book

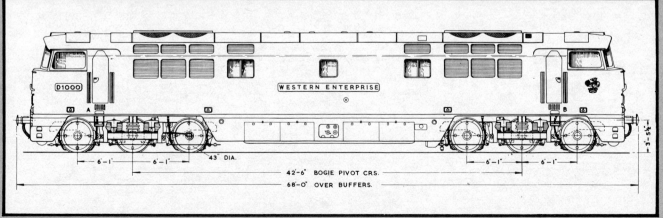

D1000 WESTERN ENTERPRISE

A          B

6'-1"   6'-1"   43" DIA.          6'-1"   6'-1"   3'-5½"

42'-6" BOGIE PIVOT CRS.

68'-0" OVER BUFFERS.

# Contents

First published 1985

ISBN 0 7110 1525 2

Published by Ian Allan Ltd, Shepperton, Surrey; and printed by Ian Allan Printing Ltd at their works at Coombelands in Runnymede, England.

## Notes for Use

● This index lists the scale drawings published in the three major model railway magazines from January 1959 to June 1985. Irish railways are included, but foreign railways are not.

● The abbreviations used for the model railway magazines are:

MRC – *Model Railway Constructor*
RM  – *Railway Modeller*
MRN – *Model Railway News* (Published until August 1971)
MRY – *Model Railways* (Published from September 1971); retitled *Your Model Railway* from October 1984

● Pre-grouping companies are listed alphabetically under the parent (post 1923) company in each major subsection (locomotives, coaches, etc.)

● Coaches have 4 wheel bogies except where indicated.

● Freight vehicles are 4 wheel except where indicated.

● Private owner wagons are excluded. These were listed in the indices published by Oakwood Press in the 1970s. Few PO wagon drawings have appeared since except for some modern vehicles which are included here in the British Railways section.

● Track plans are listed alphabetically under each parent company. The pre-grouping owner is indicated in brackets, but the track plan referenced does not necessarily correspond to the pre-grouping era.

● Following publication of a drawing, readers often send in additional information, which is published in subsequent issues. These have not been referenced here, to avoid confusion.

● The user is advised to obtain photographs of the item to be modelled. Significant modifications could occur with time.

*Cover: Chris Leigh*

*Previous page:* **Prototype 2,700hp Western Region diesel-hydraulic No D1000, *Western Enterprise*, built 1961, in its unique 'desert sand' livery. (Drawing MRC 7/71).** *British Railways (Western Region)*

**D1000 *Western Enterprise* drawing**  *R. S. Carter*

*Below:* **Ministry of Supply 2-10-0 No 73777 photographed at Cambridge in July 1945. (Drawing RM 6/83).**
*E. R. Wethersett/Ian Allan Library*

# British Railways

## Locomotives

### Steam Locomotives

| | | |
|---|---|---|
| 2-6-0 3MT | MRC | 2/82 |
| 4-6-0 4MT | MRY | 2/75 |
| 4-6-2 7P | MRY | 1/72 |
| 4-6-2 8P | MRN | 9/70 |
| | MRY | 7/81 |
| 2-8-0 Ex-War Dept | RM | 6/83 |
| 2-10-0 Ex-War Dept | RM | 6/83 |
| 2-10-0 9F (Franco-Crosti) | RM | 9/73 |
| | MRC | 2/82 |
| Tenders – Types 1, 1A-1K, 2, 2A, 3 | MRC | 5/81 |
| 2-6-2T 2MT | RM | 3/80 |
| 2-6-4T 4MT | RM | 9/83 |

### Gas Turbine Locomotives

| | | |
|---|---|---|
| 4-6-0 No GT3 | RM | 9/61 |
| | MRN | 7/62 |
| No 18000 | RM | 7/84 |

### Diesel Locomotives

| | | |
|---|---|---|
| D2950-D2952 Hunslet 0-4-0DM | MRY | 5/79 |
| Class 04 | RM | 5/81 |
| Class 05 | MRY | 8/79 |
| Class 07 | RM | 5/84 |
| Class 17 'Clayton' | RM | 6/70 |
| Class 20 | MRC | 2/82 |
| | RM | 11/82 |
| | RM | 12/82 |
| Class 23 'Baby Deltic' | RM | 5/83 |
| | RM | 6/83 |
| Class 33 | RM | 10/84 |

| | | |
|---|---|---|
| | RM | 11/84 |
| Class 35 'Hymek' | RM | 11/83 |
| Class 37 | RM | 1/83 |
| Class 40 | RM | 2/72 |
| | RM | 6/83 |
| Class 41 (D600-D604) 'Warship' | RM | 7/80 |
| Class 42 'Warship' | MRC | 10/70 |
| Class 45 | RM | 3/72 |
| Class 46 | RM | 9/83 |
| Class 47 | RM | 1/66 |
| | RM | 4/71 |
| | MRY | 8/74 |
| | RM | 4/77 |
| | MRC | 9/81 |
| Class 50 | RM | 2/68 |
| | RM | 9/82 |

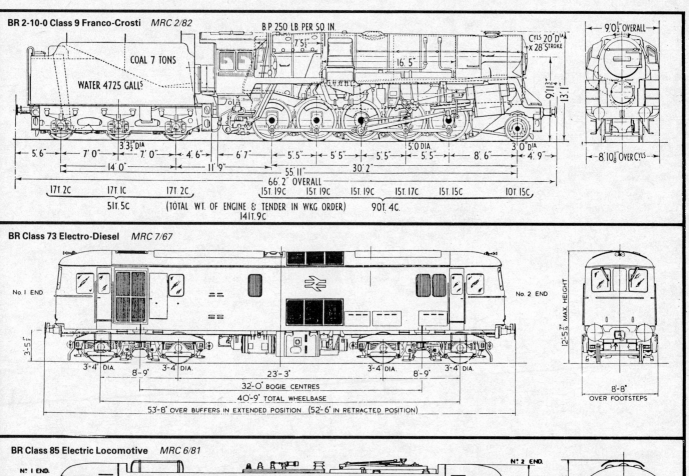

**BR 2-10-0 Class 9 Franco-Crosti** *MRC 2/82*

**BR Class 73 Electro-Diesel** *MRC 7/67*

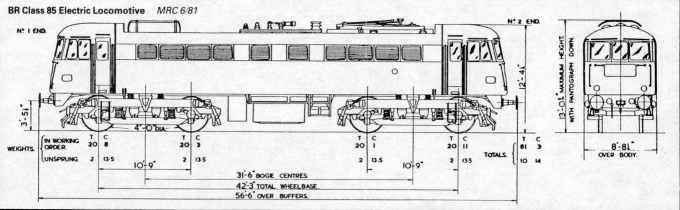

**BR Class 85 Electric Locomotive** *MRC 6/81*

## (continued listing)

Class 52 'Western' — MRC 7/71
Class 55 'Deltic' — RM 3/84
Class 56 — MRY 10/78
— RM 1/84
Class 58 — MRC 2/83

**Electric Locomotives**

20003 (SR) — MRC 11/61
— MRC 3/81
Class 71 — MRN 6/59
— MRC 11/61
— MRC 3/81
Class 73 — MRC 7/67
Class 76 — MRC 3/81
Class 81 — MRC 4/81
Class 82 — MRC 4/81
Class 83 — MRC 5/81
Class 84 — MRC 5/81
Class 85 — MRC 6/81
Class 86 — RM 1/66
— MRN 6/67
— MRC 6/81
— RM 5/85
Class 87 — MRC 7/81
— RM 2/85
Class 86 and Class 87 Bogies — MRC 3/81
Faively Pantograph — MRC 3/62

# Coaching Stock

Restaurant Buffet Car – RB(S) — MRC 8/79
Restaurant Buffet Car – RBK — MRC 8/79
Restaurant Kitchen Buffet Car – RKB — MRC 1/81
Brake Gangwayed — MRC 10/61
General Utility Van — MRC 10/61
4 wheel Covered Carriage Truck — MRC 10/61

**XP64 Stock:**
First — MRN 7/64
— RM 8/64
— MRC 9/64

Second Corridor — MRN 7/64
— RM 8/64
— MRC 9/64
Second Open — MRN 7/64
— RM 8/64
— MRC 9/64
Pullman (Euston-Manchester) Kitchen First — MRC 7/66
Pullman (Euston-Manchester) Brake First — MRC 7/66
Driving Brake Second (Edinburgh-Glasgow) — MRC 12/80
Mk 3 Coach — MRY 5/72
HM Queen's Saloon – Mk 3 — RM 8/80
HRH Duke of Edinburgh's Saloon – Mk 3 — RM 8/80
Exhibition Coaches — MRC 12/82
High Speed Recording Coach – Modified Mk2F — RM 4/83
First Semi-Open 'Silver Princess' — RM 1/80

**High Speed Train – IC125**
Power Car — RM 2/77
Trailer Restaurant Unclassified Kitchen — MRY 4/78
— MRC 1/80
Trailer Restaurant Second Buffet — MRY 4/78
— MRC 1/80
Trailer Restaurant Unclassified Buffet — MRC 1/80
Trailer Guard Second — MRC 7/82

**Diesel Multiple-Units**
'Derby Lightweight' Nos 79900/1 — MRC 1/85
Class 122 Single Railcar — RM 3/83
Birmingham RC&W 3-car Set — MRC 11/67
4 wheel Railbus (Bristol/E. Coachworks) — MRN 2/59

**Electric Multiple-Units**

**Class 309:**
Driving Trailer Composite — MRC 5/63
Motor Brake Second — MRC 5/63
Trailer Second — MRC 5/63
Driving Trailer Second — MRC 6/63
Griddle Car — MRC 6/63

**Class 310:**
Motor Brake Second — MRN 10/66
Battery Driving Trailer Second — MRN 10/66
Trailer Second — MRN 11/66
Battery Driven Trailer Composite — MRN 11/66

**Class 410 (4-BEP)**
Trailer Restaurant Buffet — MRC 10/61

**Class 420 & 421 (4-BIG & 4-CIG):**
Motor Brake Second — MRC 10/80
Trailer Second — MRC 10/80
Trailer Buffet Second — MRC 10/80
Driving Trailer Composite — MRC 10/80

**Class 430 & 491 (4-REP & 4-TC):**
Driving Motor Second — MRC 7/67
Trailer Buffet Second — MRC 7/67
Trailer Brake First — MRC 7/67
Trailer Corridor First — MRC 7/67
Trailer Brake Second — MRC 7/67
Motor Parcels Van (SR) — RM 10/61
— MRC 10/61
— MRN 7/64
De-icing Unit (SR) — MRY 9/73

# Freight Stock

12 ton Van – 4 doors — RM 2/68
12 ton Van — MRN 8/70
12 ton Van (ER) — MRN 8/70
12 ton Van (LMR) — MRN 7/70
12 ton Insulated Fish Van — MRN 12/68
12 ton Palvan — MRC 5/59

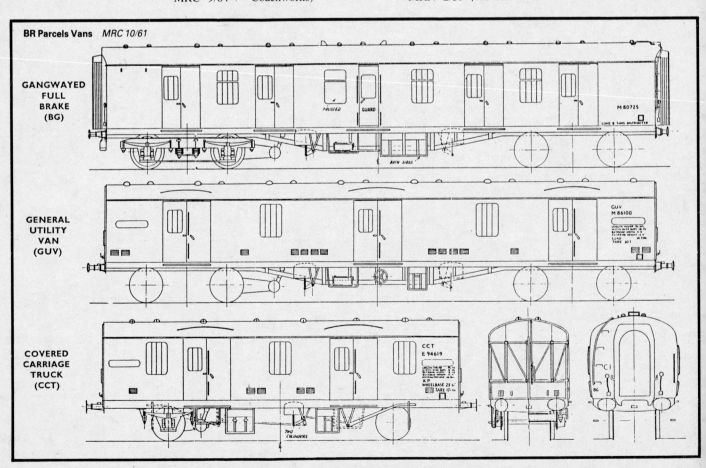

BR Parcels Vans *MRC 10/61*

GANGWAYED FULL BRAKE (BG)

GENERAL UTILITY VAN (GUV)

COVERED CARRIAGE TRUCK (CCT)

| | | | | | | | | |
|---|---|---|---|---|---|---|---|---|
| Box Van – (fitted) | MRN 12/67 | 21 ton Mineral Wagons (Rebuilt) | MRC 12/83 | Ballast Wagon, Engineers Dept. | MRC 4/64 |
| Interfrigo Van | MRC 3/67 | 22 ton Plate Wagon | MRC 5/70 | Manure Wagon (WR) | MRY 2/77 |
| Ferry Service Vans | MRC 6/63 | 26 ton Iron Ore Tippler Wagon | | British Steel Corp. Bogie | MRY 6/75 |
| | MRC 10/66 | (fitted) | RM 9/63 | ISO and Freightliner Containers | RM 8/70 |
| 20 ton Standard Goods Brake | | | RM 6/66 | Permanent Way Trolley | RM 8/65 |
| Van | MRC 5/83 | 27 ton Iron Ore Tippler | RM 9/63 | | RM 11/69 |
| 10 ton Engineers Ballast Wagon | | | RM 6/66 | | |
| 'Starfish' | MRC 3/84 | | MRN 2/67 | | |
| 12 ton Standard Pipe Wagon | MRC 4/64 | 27 ton Mineral Wagon | MRN 2/67 | | |
| 13 ton Lowfit Wagon | MRC 6/70 | 30 ton Bogie Bolster Wagons | MRC 3/83 | | |

## Structures

| | |
|---|---|
| Station – Saltaire | MRY 12/84 |
| Signal Cabin – Astley | MRC 6/83 |
| Crossing Gates | MRC 6/83 |
| Signal – Ground | MRC 1/85 |

| | | | |
|---|---|---|---|
| 13 ton China Clay Wagon (fitted) | RM 1/65 | | |
| 14 ton Engineers Ballast Wagon | | 50 ton Aggregate Wagon, | |
| 'Ling' | MRC 3/84 | Yeoman | MRY 12/77 |
| 16 ton Mineral Wagon (fitted) | MRN 11/66 | 90 ton Bogie Hopper Wagon, | |
| 16 ton Mineral Wagon (unfitted) | MRN 1/67 | Cleveland Potash | MRY 10/77 |
| 20 ton Tank Wagon – Ferry | | 50 ton Bogie Rail Wagon | |
| Traffic | MRC 11/84 | 'Salmon' | MRC 12/69 |
| 20 ton Standard Coke Hopper | | 100 ton Bogie Tank Wagon, | |
| Wagons | MRC 8/83 | Shell-Mex | MRC 8/69 |
| 20 ton Hopper Wagon | MRC 11/72 | 100 ton Bogie Procor Tank | |
| 20 ton 'Crab' Ballast Wagon | MRC 12/84 | Wagon | MRY 8/77 |
| 20 ton low-sided 'Grampus' | | Bogie Procor Tank Wagon, Esso | MRY 1/78 |
| Wagon | MRC 8/61 | Procor Tank Wagon, Conoco | MRY 9/77 |
| | MRC 3/85 | Bogie Double Deck Car Flat | |
| 20 ton Ballast Wagon 'Tunny' | MRC 3/84 | 'Cartic' | MRC 7/68 |
| 20 ton 'Lamprey' Ballast Wagon | MRC 12/84 | MGR Hopper Wagon | MRC 8/82 |
| 21 ton Mineral Wagons | MRC 11/83 | Rail Wagon (WR) | MRN 10/66 |
| | | 'Grampus' Wagon (fitted) | MRN 7/69 |

## War Department

## Locomotives

**Ministry of Supply**

| | | |
|---|---|---|
| 0-6-0ST | RM | 10/73 |
| 2-8-0 | RM | 6/83 |
| 2-10-0 | RM | 6/83 |

**US Army Transportation Corps**

| | | |
|---|---|---|
| 2-8-0 Class S160 (WW2 loan) | MRY | 3/77 |

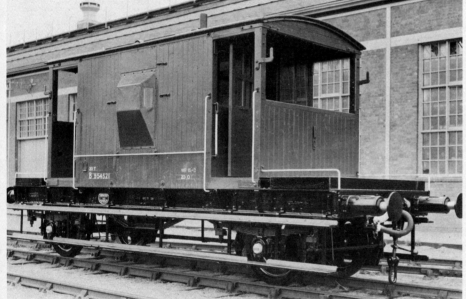

*Left:* **Standard British Railways 20 ton goods brake van No B954521, a vacuum-piped example built Darlington 1959. (Drawing MRC 5/83).**
*British Railways LM Region*

*Below:* **3,300hp Class 58 freight locomotive No 58.002 in Railfreight livery. (Drawing MRC 2/83).**
*A. Swain*

# Great Western Railway

## Locomotives

**2-2-2**

| | | |
|---|---|---|
| Nos 70-76 (1872) | RM | 8/70 |
| No 300 | MRN | 7/65 |
| Nos 378-387 (1866) | MRY | 10/83 |
| | MRY | 11/83 |
| | MRY | 12/83 |
| Firefly | MRC | 6/85 |
| Queen | MRC | 4/73 |
| 'Convertible' | MRC | 5/85 |

**4-2-2**

| | | |
|---|---|---|
| Broad Gauge | RM | 10/74 |
| | MRC | 6/85 |
| No 3077 | RM | 5/76 |

**2-4-0**

| | | |
|---|---|---|
| 'River' Class | RM | 4/69 |
| 'Avonside' Class | RM | 2/72 |
| 'Barnum' Class | RM | 7/66 |
| | MRY | 5/80 |

**4-4-0**

| | | |
|---|---|---|
| 32XX (90XX) Class 'Dukedog' | RM | 12/67 |
| | MRY | 10/72 |
| 38XX 'County' Class | RM | 10/68 |
| Armstrong | RM | 9/63 |
| 'Atbara' Class | RM | 5/71 |
| 'Badminton' Class | RM | 4/71 |
| 'Bulldog' Class | RM | 12/67 |
| 'City' Class | RM | 1/71 |
| Earl Cawdor | RM | 3/71 |
| 'Flower' Class | RM | 2/71 |
| 'Waverley' Class (Broad Gauge) | MRY | 3/82 |

**4-4-2**

| | | |
|---|---|---|
| Albion | RM | 4/68 |
| Alliance/President | MRC | 1/69 |
| | RM | 11/71 |
| | RM | 10/71 |
| La France | | |

**0-6-0**

| | | |
|---|---|---|
| Broad Gauge | MRC | 6/85 |
| 439 Class | MRY | 8/83 |
| No 908 | RM | 5/67 |
| 2251 Class | RM | 7/68 |
| 2301 Class | MRY | 11/74 |
| | RM | 11/83 |

**2-6-0**

| | | |
|---|---|---|
| 26XX 'Aberdare' Class | RM | 7/69 |
| 43XX Class | RM | 8/68 |
| 93XX Class | MRC | 11/83 |

**4-6-0**

| | | |
|---|---|---|
| No 36 (1896) | MRN | 7/59 |
| No 98 | RM | 4/68 |
| No 100 | RM | 8/68 |
| 10XX 'County' Class | RM | 11/68 |
| 29XX 'Saint' Class | RM | 4/68 |
| 4073 'Castle' Class | RM | 8/61 |
| 49XX 'Hall' Class | RM | 4/64 |
| | RM | 6/69 |
| 68XX 'Grange' Class | RM | 11/68 |
| | RM | 6/78 |
| 78XX 'Manor' Class | MRN | 11/64 |
| | RM | 6/68 |

**4-6-2**

| | | |
|---|---|---|
| Great Bear | RM | 9/70 |

**2-8-0**

| | | |
|---|---|---|
| 28XX Class | RM | 2/69 |
| | MRY | 11/71 |
| 47XX Class | RM | 2/68 |
| ROD Class | RM | 10/65 |
| | RM | 9/71 |
| | RM | 6/85 |

**Tenders**

| | | |
|---|---|---|
| 3,000 gal Churchward | RM | 1/70 |
| 3,500 gal Churchward | RM | 1/70 |
| 3,500 gal Intermediate | RM | 1/70 |
| 3,500 gal Collet | RM | 1/70 |
| 4,000 gal Collet | RM | 1/70 |
| 4,000 gal Hawksworth | RM | 1/70 |
| 4,000 gal ROD | RM | 1/70 |

**0-4-0T**

| | | |
|---|---|---|
| No 95 ex-Birkenhead Railway | MRC | 1/72 |

**0-4-2T**

| | | |
|---|---|---|
| 517 Class | MRY | 1/80 |
| | MRY | 2/80 |
| | MRY | 11/81 |
| 14XX Class | RM | 10/67 |
| | RM | 6/77 |
| 48XX Class | RM | 10/67 |
| | RM | 6/77 |
| 58XX Class | RM | 10/67 |
| | RM | 6/77 |

**2-4-0T**

| | | |
|---|---|---|
| Nos 1192/96/97 Rebuilt (ex-Cambrian Railway) | RM | 3/65 |

**2-4-2T**

| | | |
|---|---|---|
| 36XX Class | RM | 11/67 |
| | RM | 11/77 |
| No 13 (1886) | MRY | 9/83 |

**4-4-0ST**

| | | |
|---|---|---|
| Corsair (Broad Gauge) | RM | 2/73 |
| No 13 (Rebuilt from 2-4-2T) | MRY | 9/83 |

**4-4-2T**

| | | |
|---|---|---|
| 'County Tank' Class | RM | 6/71 |
| | RM | 10/84 |
| 46XX Class | RM | 2/70 |

**0-6-0T**

| | | |
|---|---|---|
| Friar Tuck (ex-Severn and Wye Railway) Broad Gauge | RM | 6/80 |
| No 704 (ex-LMMR Victory) | MRY | 8/81 |
| No 1380 | MRN | 2/70 |

**0-6-0ST**

| | | |
|---|---|---|
| 850 Class | RM | 9/68 |
| No 1751 (1701/1854 Class) | RM | 9/63 |
| 1361 Class | RM | 7/70 |

**0-6-0T/ST/PT**

| | | |
|---|---|---|
| Class 1076 (Double Framed) | RM | 7/71 |

**0-6-0ST/PT**

| | | |
|---|---|---|
| Nos 1228-1237 (1076 Class) | RM | 7/71 |

**0-6-0PT**

| | | |
|---|---|---|
| 1016 Class | RM | 5/69 |
| 1366 Class | RM | 10/67 |
| 15XX Class | RM | 3/69 |
| | MRY | 12/73 |
| | RM | 4/85 |
| 16XX Class | MRN | 2/66 |
| | RM | 7/69 |
| 19XX Class | RM | 7/73 |
| 54XX Class | MRN | 9/67 |
| | RM | 9/69 |
| 57XX Class | RM | 6/70 |
| 64XX Class | MRN | 9/67 |
| | RM | 9/69 |
| | RM | 1/80 |
| 74XX Class | MRN | 9/67 |
| | RM | 9/69 |
| 8750 Class | RM | 1/68 |
| | RM | 6/70 |
| 94XX Class | RM | 1/68 |
| | RM | 12/78 |
| 97XX Class | RM | 1/68 |
| | RM | 6/70 |

**0-6-2T**

| | | |
|---|---|---|
| 56XX Class | RM | 10/69 |
| | RM | 8/75 |
| | RM | 5/84 |

**2-6-2T**

| | | |
|---|---|---|
| 31XX Class | RM | 12/70 |
| 3150 Class | RM | 11/70 |
| 39XX Class | RM | 11/67 |
| | MRY | 4/75 |
| | RM | 4/76 |
| 44XX Class | RM | 12/68 |
| | MRY | 9/74 |
| | RM | 3/77 |
| 45XX/55XX Class | RM | 1/69 |
| | RM | 8/73 |
| | MRN | 4/70 |
| 51XX Class | RM | 10/70 |
| 61XX Class | RM | 10/70 |
| 81XX Class | RM | 12/70 |

**2-8-0T**

| | | |
|---|---|---|
| 42XX Class | RM | 3/68 |

**2-8-2T**

| | | |
|---|---|---|
| 72XX Class | RM | 12/69 |
| **Steam Railmotor** | MRN | 4/67 |

## Diesel Traction

| | | |
|---|---|---|
| 350 hp Diesel-electric (English Electric) | MRY | 4/76 |
| Diesel Railcar No 18 | MRC | 9/71 |

## Absorbed Railways

*Alexandra Docks & Railway Co*

**0-6-0T**

| | | |
|---|---|---|
| No 34 (GWR No 666) | RM | 9/66 |

*Barry Railway*

**0-6-2T**

| | | |
|---|---|---|
| Class K | MRY | 12/77 |

*Brecon & Merthyr Railway*

**0-6-0T**

| | | |
|---|---|---|
| No 35 (GWR No 2161) | RM | 9/66 |

*Bristol & Exeter Railway*

**4-2-4**

| | | |
|---|---|---|
| | RM | 12/70 |

*Cambrian Railways*

**4-4-0**

| | | |
|---|---|---|
| Sharp Stewart (1893) | MRC | 8/64 |
| | RM | 8/66 |
| Rebuilt from Metropolitan Rly | | |

**4-4-0T**

| | | |
|---|---|---|
| | RM | 2/67 |

**0-6-0**

| | | |
|---|---|---|
| Sharp Stewart | RM | 1/68 |

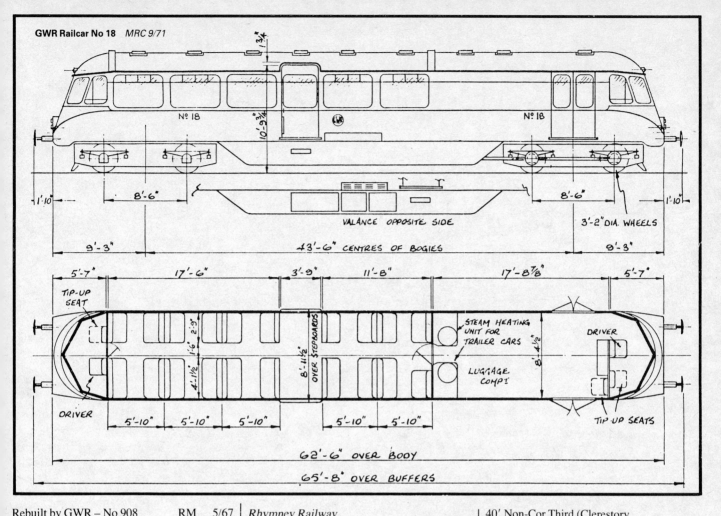

GWR Railcar No 18  *MRC 9/71*

| | | |
|---|---|---|
| Rebuilt by GWR – No 908 | RM | 5/67 |
| **0-4-0ST** | | |
| Nos 36-38, Sharp Stewart (1863) | MRY | 12/76 |
| **2-4-0T** | | |
| Rebuilt by GWR | RM | 3/65 |
| **4-4-0T** | | |
| Ex-Metropolitan Rly (Beyer Peacock) | RM | 2/67 |
| **0-6-0T** | | |
| No 13 | RM | 11/66 |

*Carmarthen & Cardigan Railway*
| | | |
|---|---|---|
| **4-4-0ST** | | |
| Broad Gauge | RM | 9/73 |

*Cleobury Mortimer & Ditton Priors Railway*
| | | |
|---|---|---|
| **0-6-0ST** | | |
| GWR Nos 28/9 | MRC | 10/71 |

*Liskeard & Caradon Railway*
| | | |
|---|---|---|
| **2-4-0T** | **MRC** | **7/66** |

*Midland & South Western Junction Railway*
| | | |
|---|---|---|
| **2-4-0** | | |
| Nos 10-12 | MRN | 3/63 |
| GWR No 1334 | RM | 5/68 |
| **2-4-0T** | | |
| No 10 (ex-SMAR) | MRN | 6/66 |
| **4-4-4T** | | |
| Nos 17/18 | RM | 3/66 |
| **0-6-0T** | | |
| Nos 1-3 (ex-SMAR) | MRN | 5/61 |
| No 4 (1894) | MRN | 4/62 |

*Port Talbot Railway*
| | | |
|---|---|---|
| **0-8-2T** | | |
| Nos 20/1 | MRY | 12/77 |

*Rhymney Railway*
| | | |
|---|---|---|
| **0-6-2T** | | |
| Sharp Stewart (1894) | MRN | 9/65 |
| No 104 | MRN | 8/63 |
| GWR No 67 | RM | 5/68 |

*Taff Vale Railway*
| | | |
|---|---|---|
| **0-6-0** | | |
| De Winton Class altered, Manning Wardle (1866) | MRY | 8/77 |
| **0-4-0T** | | |
| No 267 | MRY | 5/72 |

*Wantage Tramway*
| | | |
|---|---|---|
| **0-4-0WT** | | |
| No 5 | MRC | 11/71 |

*Weston, Clevedon & Portishead Railway*
| | | |
|---|---|---|
| **2-4-0T** | | |
| Hesperus | MRN | 12/70 |
| | MRY | 1/84 |

## Coaching Stock

*Great Western Railway*
| | | |
|---|---|---|
| 4 wheel Composite (1855) | MRC | 4/67 |
| 6 wheel – Broad Gauge | MRC | 6/85 |
| 6 wheel Parliamentary | MRN | 3/66 |
| 6 wheel Tricomposite (Diag U19) | MRC | 2/67 |
| 6 wheel Third Saloon (Diag G20) | MRC | 3/67 |
| Broad Gauge (Clerestory) | MRC | 6/85 |
| Composite (1896) | MRN | 10/69 |
| 38′6″ Suburban Brake Third | RM | 11/71 |
| 40′ Non-Cor Brake Composite (Clerestory Roof) | MRC | 10/68 |

| | | |
|---|---|---|
| 40′ Non-Cor Third (Clerestory Roof) | MRC | 11/68 |
| 40′ Brake and Luggage Vans | MRC | 3/67 |
| | MRC | 8/67 |
| | MRC | 9/67 |
| | MRC | 11/79 |
| | MRC | 1/80 |
| **48′ City Set:** | | |
| Composite | MRC | 5/62 |
| Third | MRC | 5/62 |
| Brake Third | MRC | 5/62 |
| **57′ Bow End Stock:** | | |
| Composite | MRC | 2/68 |
| Brake Composite | MRC | 1/68 |
| Brake Third | MRC | 2/68 |
| 57′ Toplight Brake Composite | MRC | 6/67 |
| 57′ Suburban Brake Third | MRC | 8/71 |
| 61′ Slipcoach (Lot 1597) | RM | 10/71 |
| 70′ Toplight Brake Third | MRY | 5/73 |
| 70′ Concertina Brake Third | RM | 3/73 |
| 70′ Restaurant Car (Lot 1219 Rebuilt) | MRC | 2/74 |
| Super Saloon | RM | 12/71 |
| | MRC | 2/73 |
| Non-Cor Brake Composite (B-Set) | MRC | 1/64 |
| Non-Cor Third – BPGV Line (1939) | MRC | 10/63 |
| Non-Cor Brake Third – BPGV Line (1939) | MRC | 10/63 |
| Royal Train Set | MRC | 4-8/73 |
| | MRC | 12/73 |
| Diamond Jubilee Royal Train Set | MRC | 4-6/81 |
| | MRC | 8/81 |
| Railmotor Auto Coach | MRN | 4/67 |

Mail Van – Clerestory Roof (Broad Gauge) RM 10/74
50' 'Monster' Van – outside framing (Diag P16) RM 12/67
50' 'Monster' Van – inside framing (Diag P18) RM 12/67
Covered Motor Car Truck – DAMO 'A' MRC 2/71
Covered Motor Car Truck – DAMO 'B' MRC 2/71
Covered Motor Car Truck – ASMO MRC 2/71
Horsebox (1876) MRC 4/72
8' Equalising Beam Bogie MRC 11/60

*Barry Railway*
6 wheel Composite MRC 12/63
6 wheel Third MRC 12/63
6 wheel Full Brake MRC 12/63

*Brecon & Merthyr Railway*
4 wheel Composite MRC 12/63
4 wheel Third MRC 12/63
4 wheel Brake Third MRC 12/63

*Bristol & Gloucester Railway*
6 wheel Parliamentary MRN 3/66

*Cambrian Railways*
4 wheel First Saloon MRY 11/77
6 wheel Coaches MRC 9/64
6 wheel Family Saloon MRY 9/77
6 wheel Football Saloon MRY 9/77
6 wheel Observation Coach MRC 11/64

*Rhymney Railway*
6 wheel Covered Carriage Truck MRC 10/64

*Taff Vale Railway*
Composite MRC 6/67
Third MRC 12/67

*Weston Clevedon & Portishead Railway*
Coach MRN 4/70

# Freight Stock

*Great Western Railway*
8 ton Van MRN 2/66

10 ton Covered Van MRC 5/66
10 ton Banana Van 'Fruit B' MRN 1/68
10 ton Gunpowder Van MRN 4/60
20 ton Covered Van MRC 3/69
30 ton Ventilated Van MRN 3/66
'Mink' Vans RM 1/79
'Mink A' Van MRC 6/62
MRC 2/63
MRC 11/73
'Mink F' Bogie Van MRC 10/84
'Mink G' Van MRC 7/73
Explosives Van MRN 10/67
Covered Goods Van MRC 6/65
Cattle Vans RM 8/78
6 wheel Fish Van MRC 1/67
Brake Vans (1880-1950) MRC 5/76
MRC 7/76
12 ton Brake Van MRN 8/62
6 wheel Brake Van MRC 10/62
Broad Gauge Wagons MRC 6/85
8 ton Open Wagon MRN 2/66
10 ton Open Wagon MRN 2/66
10 ton Mineral Wagon RM 3/62
10 ton medium-sided Goods Wagon RM 12/79
10 ton high-sided Goods Wagon RM 1/80
12 ton Roll Wagon MRC 12/64
14 ton Open Goods Wagon RM 7/79
21 ton Mineral Wagon RM 9/78
Double Bolster Timber Wagon 'Macaw A' MRC 10/65
Slate Wagon Transporter MRC 2/66
Tilt Wagon (Broad Gauge) RM 10/74
Timber Truck (Broad Gauge) RM 10/74
Gas Cylinder Wagon MRC 4/64
Oil and Gas Wagons MRC 12/65
Tool Van MRC 1/60
Shunting Truck (1909) MRC 2/63
Dean – Churchward Wagon Brake Gear MRC 6/62

*Alexandra Docks Railway*
10 ton low-sided Open Wagon MRN 5/66

*Barry Railway*
10 ton Van MRN 1/66
RM 4/78
Brake Van MRC 3/61
10 ton Goods Wagon with Trestle RM 1/78
RM 3/79

10 ton Goods Wagon with Catch Trestle RM 11/77

*Brecon & Merthyr Railway*
8 ton low-dropsided Wagon RM 10/77
2 plank Open Wagon MRN 12/60
Ballast Wagon RM 9/83

*Cambrian Railways*
6 ton Van MRC 12/62
15 ton Brake Van MRC 10/62
8 ton low-dropsided Wagon MRN 12/65
10 ton high-sided Goods Wagon RM 12/78

*Cleobury Mortimer & Ditton Priors Railway*
8 ton Open Wagon MRN 7/59

*Midland & South Western Junction Railway*
8 ton Van – Fitted MRN 12/61
10 ton Goods Van RM 6/75
10 ton high-sided Wagon MRC 5/70
10 ton Flat/Furniture Wagon RM 4/77
10 ton Trolley Wagon MRN 8/63
10 ton Single Bolster Wagon RM 12/76
Single Bolster Wagon – Dumb Buffers RM 7/77

*Port Talbot Railway*
Open Wagon MRN 7/60

*Rhondda & Swansea Bay Railway*
Van MRN 1/66

*Rhymney Railway*
6 ton Brake Van MRC 2/62
14 ton Brake Van MRC 12/59
8 ton Goods Wagon RM 4/76
10 ton low-sided Goods Wagon RM 10/76
10 ton low-sided Goods Wagon with Centre Doors RM 9/78

*Taff Vale Railway*
10 ton Goods Van MRC 3/64
RM 6/79
10 ton Iron Goods Van RM 3/78
10 ton Mineral Wagon RM 9/61
10 ton high-sided Goods Wagon RM 6/74
10 ton low-sided Goods Wagon RM 10/75
RM 11/76
10 ton drop-sided Wagon RM 9/61
10 ton Mineral Wagon RM 9/61
10 ton Tarpaulin Wagon RM 9/61

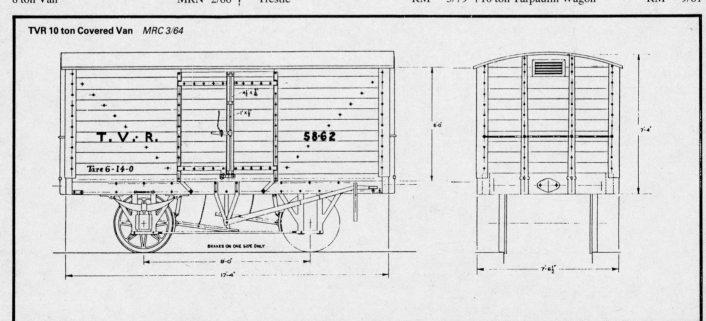

**TVR 10 ton Covered Van** *MRC 3/64*

T.V.R. 5862 Tare 6-14-0
4½ x ⅝  1'x1½
BRAKES ON ONE SIDE ONLY
9'-0"  17'-4"  6'-0"  7'-4"  7'-6½"

# Structures

*Great Western Railway*

**Stations:**

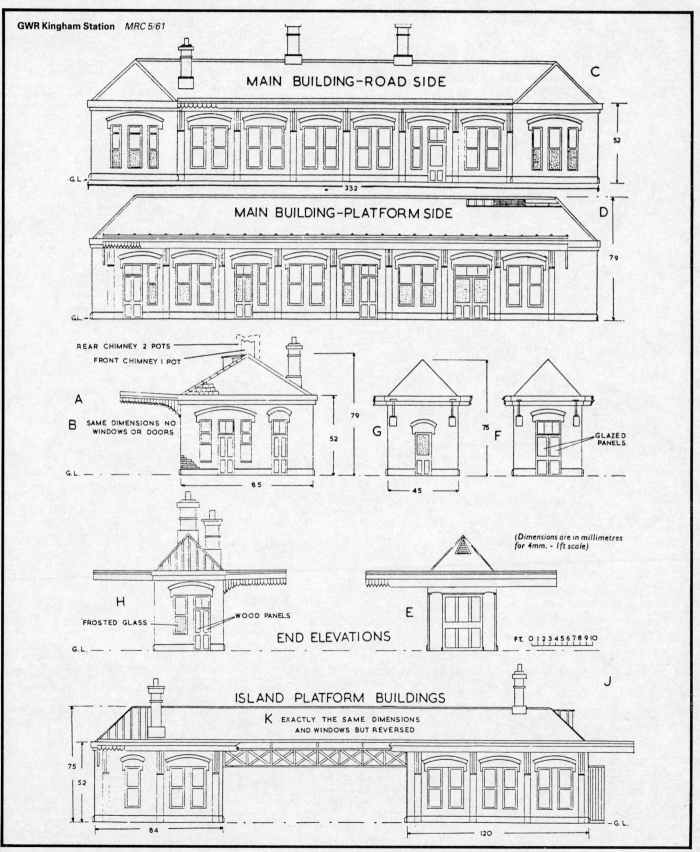

GWR Kingham Station   MRC 5/61

MAIN BUILDING-ROAD SIDE   C

52

G.L.   332

MAIN BUILDING-PLATFORM SIDE   D

79

G.L.

A
REAR CHIMNEY 2 POTS
FRONT CHIMNEY 1 POT
B  SAME DIMENSIONS NO WINDOWS OR DOORS
79
52
G.L.
85

G  75  F   GLAZED PANELS
45

H
FROSTED GLASS   WOOD PANELS
G.L.

E
END ELEVATIONS

(Dimensions are in millimetres for 4mm. - 1ft scale)

FT. 0 1 2 3 4 5 6 7 8 9 10

ISLAND PLATFORM BUILDINGS

K  EXACTLY THE SAME DIMENSIONS AND WINDOWS BUT REVERSED

J

75
52
G.L.
84   120

| | |
|---|---|
| Notgrove | MRN 5/62 |
| Parkend | MRC 6/81 |
| Plympton | RM 5/69 |
| Praze | MRN 3/67 |
| Ross-on-Wye | MRC 7/63 |
| St Briavels | RM 5/60 |
| St Erth | RM 5/85 |
| South Leigh | RM 10/78 |
| Staverton Bridge | RM 7/70 |
| Stonehouse | RM 8/77 |
| Thorn | RM 5/69 |
| Uffculme | RM 7/77 |
| Upwey | RM 2/68 |
| Wallingford | RM 11/79 |
| Witney | RM 6/78 |
| Wrington | RM 9/65 |
| Stations – Brunel Types | MRC 7/83 |
| | MRC 8/83 |
| | MRC 8/84 |
| Station Waiting Room | MRC 7/83 |
| Station Master's House | MRC 7/83 |
| Station Valance | MRN 2/62 |
| Station Nameboard | MRN 1/62 |
| | MRC 8/77 |
| Station Footbridge | MRC 2/69 |
| | MRC 4/71 |
| | MRC 4/77 |
| Platform Seat | MRC 10/66 |
| Oil Lamp | MRC 11/64 |
| | MRC 12/65 |
| Gas Lamp | MRC 12/65 |
| **Signalboxes:** | |
| Andoversford | MRC 3/62 |
| Bodmin | MRC 1/84 |
| Deeside Loop | MRC 2/73 |
| Drws-y-Nant | MRC 2/73 |
| Gara Bridge | RM 6/68 |
| Hatch | RM 5/69 |
| Ilminster | RM 6/69 |
| Maiden Newton | MRC 8/77 |
| | RM 12/79 |
| Montacute | RM 4/60 |
| Moretonhampstead | RM 9/60 |
| Newton Abbot East | MRC 9/79 |
| Radstock West | MRY 4/76 |
| Ross-on-Wye | MRC 11/64 |
| St Erth | RM 6/85 |
| Staverton Bridge | RM 7/70 |
| Stonehouse | RM 8/77 |
| Stow-on-the-Wold | RM 7/61 |
| Toddington | MRC 5/82 |
| Torre | MRC 3/68 |
| Signalbox – Standard Type | MRN 6/69 |
| | MRY 4/82 |
| Ground Frame | MRN 3/67 |
| Token Apparatus | RM 4/60 |
| | MRN 3/62 |
| | RM 9/66 |
| | MRC 11/69 |
| **Goods Sheds:** | |
| Bodmin | MRC 6/84 |
| Buckfastleigh | RM 6/68 |
| Chudleigh | MRC 2/73 |
| Chipping Campden | MRN 12/62 |
| Hatch | RM 5/69 |
| Helston | MRN 10/67 |
| Highworth | MRN 10/66 |
| Ilminster | RM 6/69 |
| Lampeter | RM 9/73 |
| Loddiswell | MRY 6/77 |
| Maiden Newton | MRC 8/77 |
| Parkend | MRC 6/81 |
| Princess Risborough | MRY 12/83 |
| Ross-on-Wye | MRC 1/63 |
| St Erth | RM 6/85 |
| Taplow | MRC 7/62 |
| Thame | MRY 7/75 |
| Broad Gauge Type | RM 5/74 |
| Large Type | RM 7/80 |
| Stone Type | RM 1/73 |
| Timber Type | MRN 2/62 |
| Weighbridge | MRN 6/63 |
| Weigh Office | RM 5/69 |
| | MRC 1/84 |
| Cattle Dock | RM 5/69 |
| Goods Yard Crane | RM 5/69 |
| | RM 6/69 |
| Yard Lamps | MRN 9/62 |
| **Loco Sheds:** | |
| Ashburton | MRC 10/75 |
| Helston | MRN 9/67 |
| Moretonhampstead | RM 9/60 |
| Ross-on-Wye | MRC 5/63 |
| Tetbury | RM 1/68 |
| Coal Stage | RM 2/80 |
| Bucket Coaling Stage | RM 1/59 |
| Turntable | MRN 6/62 |
| Carriage Shed | MRN 9/67 |
| Store | MRN 9/67 |
| | RM 6/68 |
| Lamp Hut | RM 7/70 |
| | MRC 4/84 |
| P/W Trolley Hut | RM 5/69 |
| | RM 11/69 |
| Platelayers Hut | RM 3/80 |
| Hut, Corrugated Iron | MRN 3/66 |
| Bicycle Shed | MRC 4/64 |
| Bridge, Stone/Brick (Broad Gauge) | MRC 1/80 |
| Bridge, Timber (Broad Gauge) | MRC 2/80 |
| Bridge | MRC 9/81 |
| Viaduct | MRN 5/59 |
| | MRC 2/63 |
| | RM 10/69 |
| Viaduct (Broad Gauge) | MRC 3/80 |
| Water Tank | MRC 8/64 |
| | RM 10/66 |
| Conical Water Tank | MRC 11/63 |
| | MRC 4/82 |
| Water Column | MRN 8/62 |
| | MRC 3/64 |
| | RM 9/68 |
| Crossing Gates | MRC 8/65 |
| Buffer Stops | MRC 9/65 |
| **Signals:** | |
| Starting | MRC 7/82 |
| | MRC 8/82 |
| Main | MRC 7/82 |
| Arms | RM 9/65 |
| | MRC 8/82 |
| Subsidiary | RM 2/66 |
| Signs and Warning Board | RM 5/66 |
| Ground | MRC 1/85 |
| Summary | MRC 1/84 |
| *Barry Railway* | |
| Loco Shed – Bridgend | MRY 4/77 |
| | MRY 5/77 |
| Coal Stage | MRY 5/77 |
| Signal Finial | MRN 12/62 |
| Signals Summary | MRC 1/84 |
| *Cardiff Railway* | |
| Masonry Bridge | MRN 4/64 |
| *Cambrian Railway* | |
| Marchwiel Station | MRC 9/68 |
| Signalbox – Newbridge-on-Wye | MRY 4/74 |
| Signal Finial | MRN 9/63 |
| Signal – Ground | MRC 1/85 |
| Signals Summary | MRC 1/84 |
| *Midland & South Western Junction Railway* | |
| Signalbox – Cricklade | MRN 1/69 |

**GWR Conical Water Tower** *MRC 4/82*

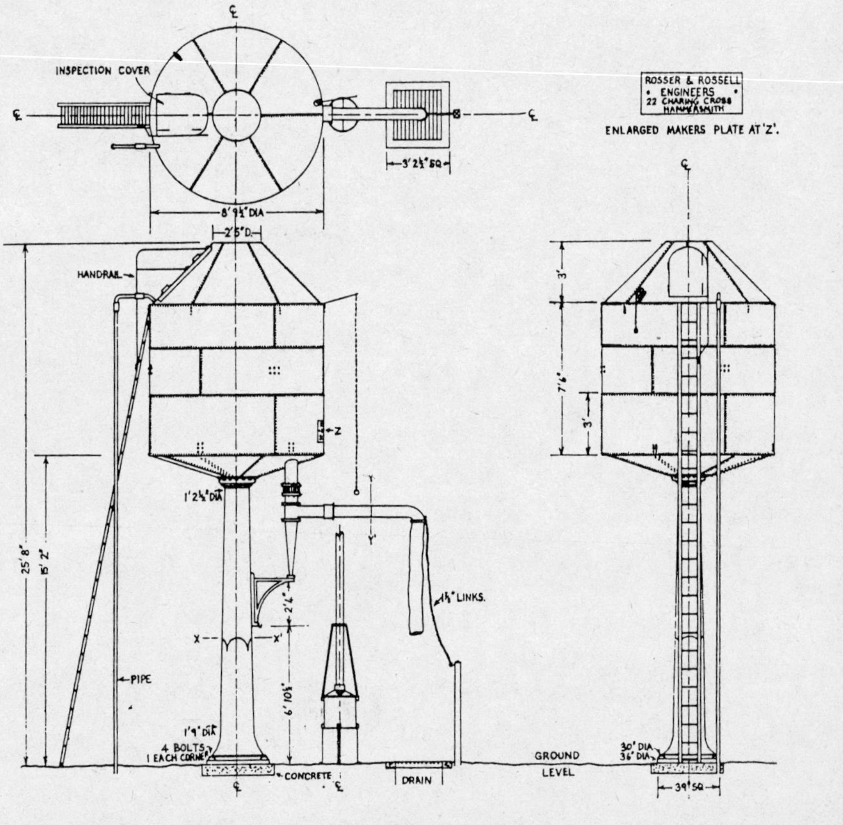

*Below:* **Great Western Railway signalbox and locomotive shed at Moretonhampstead. (Drawing RM 9/60).** *N. L. M. Stone*

# London, Midland & Scottish Railway

## Locomotives

**4-4-0**

| | | |
|---|---|---|
| Class 2P | RM | 12/84 |
| | RM | 5/85 |

**2-6-0**

| | | |
|---|---|---|
| 64XX Class 2 | MRY | 1/73 |
| | RM | 4/82 |
| Class 4 'Crab' | MRY | 9/73 |
| Stanier | RM | 1/72 |

**4-6-0**

| | | |
|---|---|---|
| Proposed Modified 'Prince of Wales' | MRY | 8/78 |
| 'Royal Scot' Class – Unrebuilt | RM | 11/60 |
| 'Royal Scot' Class – *Fury* | RM | 10/81 |
| 'Patriot' Class | RM | 9/68 |
| 'Jubilee' Class | RM | 12/65 |
| | MRY | 6/74 |
| 'Jubilee' Class Nos 5665-5742 | MRY | 2/76 |
| 'Jubilee' Tenders: | | |
|    3,500 gal Tender | RM | 1/66 |
| | MRY | 1/74 |
|    3,500 gal Fowler Tender | MRY | 6/74 |
| | RM | 1/72 |
|    4,000 gal Stanier Tender | MRY | 6/74 |
| Class 5 | MRY | 12/73 |

**4-6-2**

| | | |
|---|---|---|
| 'Turbomotive' No 6202 | MRN | 7/68 |

**0-4-0ST**

| | | |
|---|---|---|
| Kitson Nos 7000-7004 | MRC | 5/60 |

**0-4-0T**

| | | |
|---|---|---|
| Sentinel | MRC | 5/64 |

**0-6-0T**

| | | |
|---|---|---|
| Standard Class 3F | MRN | 1/71 |
| | RM | 5/80 |

**2-6-2T**

| | | |
|---|---|---|
| Class 3 Nos 1-70 | RM | 1/65 |

**2-6-4T**

| | | |
|---|---|---|
| Class 4 Nos 2537-2672 | RM | 5/66 |

**2-6-6-2T**

| | | |
|---|---|---|
| Beyer-Garratt | RM | 10/68 |

**Sentinel Railcar 100hp**   MRY   9/79

**3,000 gal Tender**   RM   9/68

**Corridor Tender – Mobile Test Train**   MRC   5/63

**Attachments**

| | | |
|---|---|---|
| Push-Pull Fittings | RM | 8/64 |
| Snowplough Class 4F | RM | 12/67 |

**Diesel Shunters**

350hp Diesel-electric Shunter:

| | | |
|---|---|---|
| Armstrong Whitworth No 7058 | MRY | 10/74 |
| English Electric Nos 7069-78 | MRY | 8/75 |
| English Electric No 7079 | MRY | 4/76 |
| English Electric Nos 7120-25 | MRY | 6/76 |
| Hunslet Diesel-Mechanical (1932) | RM | 1/71 |

**Steam Cranes**

| | | |
|---|---|---|
| Walker Cruiser 6 ton Crane | MRC | 5/83 |
| Cowans Sheldon 50 ton Breakdown Crane | MRY | 10/72 |

## Absorbed Railways

*Caledonian Railway*

**2-4-0**

| | | |
|---|---|---|
| Conner (1878) | MRN | 1/63 |

**4-4-0**

| | | |
|---|---|---|
| 'Oban Bogie' | RM | 3/74 |
| Nos 13-18 | RM | 2/66 |
| Drummond (1888) | RM | 10/70 |
| 'Dunalastair III' | RM | 3/70 |
| 'Dunalastair IV' – Saturated and Superheated | MRC | 3/78 |

**0-6-0**

| | | |
|---|---|---|
| Neilson (1868) | MRN | 11/65 |

**4-6-0**

| | | |
|---|---|---|
| Class 55 | RM | 1/66 |
| Class 60 | RM | 3/69 |

**0-4-2T**

| | | |
|---|---|---|
| Nos 262-263 | RM | 10/66 |

**0-4-4T**

| | | |
|---|---|---|
| Class 19 | RM | 3/72 |

**0-6-0T**

| | | |
|---|---|---|
| 'Jubilee Pug' | MRY | 7/75 |

**0-8-0T**

| | | |
|---|---|---|
| Class 492 | RM | 3/77 |

**Tenders**

| | | |
|---|---|---|
| 4,300 gal McIntosh | MRC | 3/78 |
| 4,600 gal McIntosh | MRC | 3/78 |

**15 ton Steam Breakdown Crane**   MRC   3/72

*Furness Railway*

**0-4-0**

| | | |
|---|---|---|
| No 3 | RM | 3/63 |
| Nos 17-20, 25-26 | RM | 11/66 |

**2-4-0**

| | | |
|---|---|---|
| No 44a | RM | 8/67 |

**4-4-0**

| | | |
|---|---|---|
| Sharp Stewart (1896) | RM | 8/66 |
| Nos 120-123 | MRN | 7/62 |
| | RM | 3/64 |
| Class K3 | RM | 5/67 |
| Class K4 | RM | 5/67 |

**0-6-0**

| | | |
|---|---|---|
| Nos 3-6 | RM | 6/65 |
| No 58 | MRN | 12/64 |
| Class D1 | RM | 1/68 |
| Class D5 | MRY | 6/75 |

**2-2-2T**

| | | |
|---|---|---|
| | RM | 11/65 |
| | RM | 12/68 |
| | RM | 2/72 |

**0-4-0ST**

| | | |
|---|---|---|
| Rebuilt from 0-4-0 | RM | 11/66 |
| Sharp Stewart (1864) | RM | 11/67 |

**2-4-2T**

| | | |
|---|---|---|
| Nos 47/8 and 70-74 | RM | 11/65 |

**4-4-2T**

| | | |
|---|---|---|
| Nos 38-43 | MRN | 9/61 |
| | MRC | 3/63 |
| | RM | 12/65 |

**0-6-0T**

| | | |
|---|---|---|
| Class G1 | RM | 11/66 |
| Class G1 Rebuild | RM | 11/66 |
| Class G5 | RM | 6/67 |
| Nos 82/3 | MRY | 8/84 |

**0-6-2T**

| | | |
|---|---|---|
| Class L1 | RM | 4/67 |
| Class L2 | RM | 7/67 |
| Class L4 | RM | 4/67 |
| | RM | 9/83 |
| Nos 96/7, 108-111 | RM | 6/65 |
| Nos 103-107 | MRN | 4/61 |

**4-6-4T**

| | | |
|---|---|---|
| Nos 115-119 | RM | 4/66 |
| | RM | 1/77 |

*Glasgow & South Western Railway*

**0-4-2**

| | | |
|---|---|---|
| Class 221 | MRN | 6/61 |

**4-4-0**

| | | |
|---|---|---|
| Class 119 | RM | 3/75 |

**4-6-0**

| | | |
|---|---|---|
| No 128 | RM | 3/71 |

**0-4-0T**

| | | |
|---|---|---|
| | RM | 5/64 |

**0-6-2T**

| | | |
|---|---|---|
| Class 1 | RM | 2/77 |
| Class 45 | RM | 2/77 |

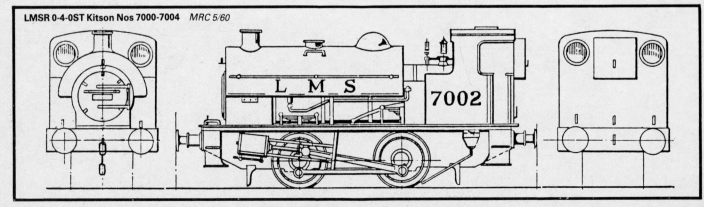

**LMSR 0-4-0ST Kitson Nos 7000-7004**   *MRC 5/60*

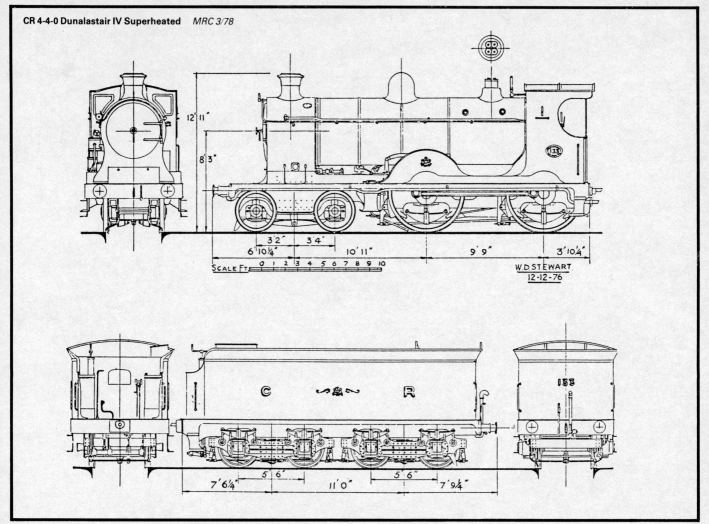

| | | | | | | |
|---|---|---|---|---|---|---|
| **4-6-4T** | | | **2-4-0CT** | | **2-4-0T** | |
| Class 540 | MRN | 9/64 | Crane Tank | MRC 6/60 | 'Chopper Tank' | MRC 12/72 |
| | RM | 7/75 | **2-4-2T** | RM 10/67 | **2-4-2T** | |
| **15 ton Breakdown Crane** | MRC | 5/71 | | MRN 3/69 | 'Precursor Tank' | RM 7/68 |
| | | | | MRY 1/84 | | RM 1/72 |
| *Highland Railway* | | | **0-4-4T** | | **0-6-2T** | |
| **4-4-0** | | | Barton Wright (1877) | MRN 11/62 | 'Watford Tank' | RM 5/69 |
| 'Small Ben' Class | MRC | 3/80 | **4-wheel Bogie – Swing Link** | MRY 10/75 | | RM 7/73 |
| 'Small Ben' Class (LMS rebuilt) | MRC | 4/80 | | | 'Coal Tank' | MRY 11/75 |
| 'Durn' Class | MRC | 1/76 | | | | RM 2/82 |
| 'Large Ben' Class | RM | 7/76 | *London & North Western Railway* | | **4-6-2T** | MRN 6/65 |
| **4-6-0** | | | **2-2-2** | | | RM 9/66 |
| 'Clan' Class | MRC | 8/78 | *Planet* (Liverpool & Manchester | | **Railmotor** | MRC 2/69 |
| 'Big Goods' Class | MRN | 2/61 | Railway) | RM 12/69 | **Daimler Railcar** | MRN 12/68 |
| | MRY | 12/72 | **4-2-0** | | **18in Gauge** | |
| 'Superheated Goods' Class | MRC | 11/74 | Crampton Courier (1847) | MRY 7/84 | *Pet* Crewe Works (1865) | RM 9/75 |
| **2-2-2T** | | | **2-4-0** | | | |
| No. 12 *Strathpeffer* | MRN | 3/60 | 'Jumbo' | MRN 3/69 | *London, Tilbury & Southend Railway* | |
| **0-4-0T** | | | 'Whitworth' | MRN 6/67 | **4-4-2T** | |
| *Strathpeffer* (1901 rebuilt) | MRY | 9/71 | **2-4-2** | | 'Tilbury Tank' | MRN 5/65 |
| **0-4-4T** | | | 'Greater Britain' | MRN 1/65 | | MRC 12/75 |
| *Strathpeffer (1890)* | | | 'John Hick' | MRN 1/66 | | RM 8/82 |
| | *MRY* | *9/71* | **4-4-0** | | Class 79 | RM 12/61 |
| **4-4-0T** | | | 'Jubilee' | MRY 2/79 | | |
| No 17 *Aberfeldy* | MRC | 12/60 | **0-6-0** | | *Maryport & Carlisle Railway* | |
| **0-6-4T** | | | 'Cauliflower' | MRN 6/70 | **2-4-0** | |
| Class 39 | MRC | 2/77 | **4-6-0** | | Crompton | MRN 5/66 |
| **15 ton Breakdown Crane** | MRC | 7/70 | 'Claughton' | RM 3/85 | **0-4-2** | |
| | | | 'Prince of Wales' | MRY 5/75 | No 4 | RM 2/65 |
| *Lancashire & Yorkshire Railway* | | | **0-8-0** | | **0-6-0** | |
| **4-4-0** | | | G1 | RM 10/69 | Nos 29/30 | RM 4/71 |
| Nos 813-842 | MRN | 8/61 | | RM 11/69 | | RM 9/76 |
| **4-4-2** | | | | MRN 12/70 | **0-4-2T** | |
| | RM | 2/85 | | MRY 7/73 | No 17 | RM 2/65 |

| 0-4-4T | | |
| No 26 | MRC | 4/60 |
| | MRY | 5/84 |

*Midland Railway*
| 4-2-2 | | |
| 'Spinner' | RM | 9/65 |
| | MRY | 9/79 |
| 0-4-0 | | |
| Ex-Leicester & Swannington | | |
| Railway (1832) | MRY | 6/75 |
| 2-4-0 | | |
| No 1400 | MRN | 12/61 |
| 4-4-0 | | |
| *Beatrice* (1885) | RM | 4/65 |
| Class 2 Superheated | MRY | 12/75 |
| 0-6-0 | | |
| No 202 (1850) | MRY | 4/79 |
| Class M | MRN | 3/61 |
| No 3130 | MRY | 2/74 |
| Class 3F | RM | 6/64 |
| | RM | 7/64 |
| Class 4F | RM | 11/63 |
| | RM | 1/67 |
| 2-6-0 | | |
| Baldwin | RM | 5/85 |
| 0-10-0 | | |
| 'Big Bertha' | RM | 10/67 |
| | RM | 11/67 |
| 0-4-4T | | |
| Class 1P | MRN | 12/62 |
| | MRY | 6/73 |
| **0-6-0T** | | |
| Class 1F | MRN | 2/63 |
| | MRY | 1/75 |
| | MRY | 10/75 |
| Class 3F | RM | 10/64 |
| | RM | 3/67 |
| | RM | 11/68 |
| **0-6-4T** | | |
| Class 3P 'Flatiron' | MRN | 3/64 |
| **6-wheel Tenders – Johnson** | MRY | 12/75 |
| **Large Snowplow – Settle &** | | |
| **Carlisle** | MRN | 12/65 |

*North London Railway*
| **4-4-0T** | | |
| Class 51 (1865) | MRY | 9/83 |
| | RM | 12/71 |
| **4-wheel Bogie – Adams** | MRY | 9/75 |

*North Staffordshire Railway*
| **2-4-0** | | |
| Nos 15, 54 | RM | 6/66 |
| **0-6-4T** | | |
| Class C | MRC | 7/62 |
| Class F | MRC | 7/62 |

*Wirral Railway*
| **4-4-4T** | | |
| No 11 | MRN | 12/67 |
| No 14 | MRC | 2/61 |

*Somerset & Dorset Joint Railway*
| **4-4-0** | | |
| Johnson (1896) | RM | 6/68 |
| **0-6-0** | | |
| No 20 | MRY | 4/82 |
| **2-8-0** | | |
| Fowler (1914) | RM | 2/67 |
| | MRY | 6/72 |
| **0-4-0T** | | |
| Sentinel | MRY | 3/75 |
| **0-4-4T** | | |
| Nos 10-13, 52-55 | MRN | 12/66 |
| No 10 (Rebuilt) | MRN | 2/67 |
| No 13 (Rebuilt) | MRN | 1/67 |

## Coaching Stock

*London Midland & Scottish Railway*
**Corridor Stock:**
| First (Diag 1747) | MRC | 12/66 |
| First (Diag 1748) | MRC | 10/66 |
| Composite (Diag 1694) | MRC | 9/66 |
| Composite (Diag 1716) | MRC | 10/66 |
| | RM | 9/68 |
| Composite (Diags 1925 & | | |
| 2159) | RM | 1/69 |
| | RM | 3/69 |
| Third (Diag 1782) | MRC | 12/67 |
| Third (Diag 1899) | RM | 7/66 |
| Brake First (Diag 1654) | MRC | 12/67 |
| Brake First (Diag 1717) | MRC | 12/67 |
| | RM | 9/68 |
| Brake Composite (Diag 1720) | RM | 7/68 |
| Brake Composite (Diag 1755) | MRC | 12/66 |
| Brake Composite (Diags 1932 | | |
| & 2010) | RM | 3/69 |
| Brake Third (Diag 1696) | MRC | 9/66 |
| | RM | 11/68 |
| Brake Third (Diag 1905) | RM | 6/66 |

**Vestibule Stock:**
| First (Diag 1707) | RM | 11/67 |
| First (Diag 1719) | MRC | 12/67 |
| Composite (Diag 1903) | RM | 11/66 |
| Third (Diag 1745) | MRC | 1/66 |
| Third (Diag 1807) | RM | 5/68 |
| Third (Diag 1904) | RM | 9/66 |
| First Brake Lounge (Diag | | |
| 1741) | RM | 11/67 |
| Brake Third (Diag 1746) | MRC | 1/66 |
| 12 wheel Composite Dining | | |
| Car (Diag 1811) | RM | 3/68 |
| 12 wheel Third Dining Car | | |
| (Diags 1901 & 1923) | RM | 1/68 |
| 12 wheel Composite Sleeping | | |
| Car (Diag 1781) | RM | 7/67 |

**Non Corridor Stock:**
| Composite (Diag 1701) | RM | 1/67 |
| Composite (Diag 1734) | RM | 4/65 |
| Third (Diag 1700) | RM | 1/67 |
| Third (Diag 1784) | RM | 5/65 |
| Brake Third (Diag 1703) | RM | 3/67 |
| Brake Third (Diag 1735) | RM | 2/66 |
| Push-Pull Brake Third (Diag | | |
| 1790) | RM | 11/64 |
| Interdistrict Set | MRC | 10/65 |

**Royal Train:**
| King's and Queen's Saloon | MRC | 7/69 |
| Dining Car | MRC | 8/69 |
| Semi-Royal | MRC | 9/69 |
| Sleeping Car | MRC | 10/69 |
| Brake First | MRC | 12/69 |
| Full Brake Van (Diag 1715) | MRC | 4/65 |

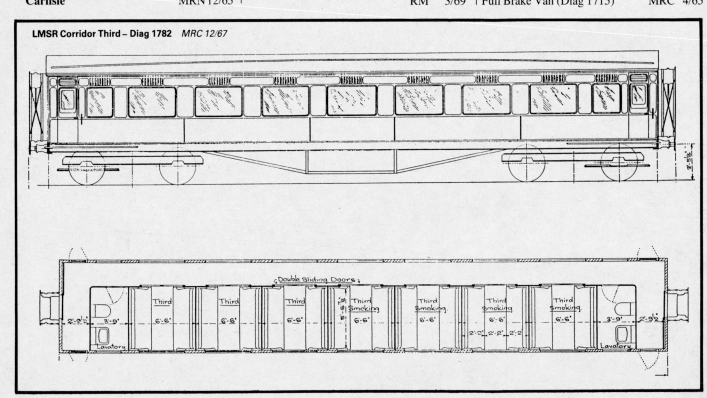

**LMSR Corridor Third – Diag 1782** *MRC 12/67*

## West Coast Joint Stock / LMS Prototype listings

| Item | Reference |
|---|---|
| Full Brake Van (Diag 1778) | MRC 4/65 |
|  | RM 5/67 |
| 6 wheel Full Brake Van | MRC 6/65 |
| Parcels Van (Diag 1870) | RM 7/64 |
| 4 wheel Fish Van (Diag 1885) | RM 1/64 |
| 6 wheel Fish Van (Diag 2115) | RM 11/69 |
| 6 wheel Milk Van (Diag 1874) | RM 1/70 |
| 6 wheel Insulated Milk Van (Diag 1936) | RM 10/66 |
| 6 wheel Palethorpe's Sausage Van (Diag 1955) | RM 12/66 |
| 6 wheel Covered Combination Truck (Diag 1872) | RM 3/70 |
| 4 wheel Open Carriage Truck (Diag 2027) | MRC 8/61 |
| 4 wheel Horse Box (Diag 1956) | MRY 11/76 |

**Inspection Saloons:**

| Item | Reference |
|---|---|
| No 45002 (ex-LNWR Director's Saloon) | MRY 5/74 |
| No 45010 (ex-MR Superintendent's Railmotor) | MRY 11/74 |
| No 45019 (ex-GSWR Director's Saloon) | MRY 2/76 |
| No 45022 (ex-LNWR Director's Saloon) | MRY 8/74 |
| No 45025 (ex-LNWR Family Saloon) | MRY 11/73 |
| No 45038 (ex-LYR Superintendent's Saloon) | MRY 12/75 |
| No 45040 (ex-NSR Inspection Saloon) | MRY 1/75 |
| No 45041 (ex-NSR Inspection Saloon) | MRY 4/75 |
| No 45042 (ex-HR Director's Saloon) | MRY 6/75 |
| Sleeping Van, S & T Dept (ex-LNWR Composite Sleeping Car) | MRC 7/74 |

*West Coast Joint Stock*
**50' Arc Roof Corridor Stock:**

| Item | Reference |
|---|---|
| Composite (Diag 30) | MRC 9/71 |
| Third (Diag 51) | MRC 9/71 |
| Brake First (Diag 18) | MRC 9/71 |
| Brake Composite (Diag 42) | MRC 9/71 |
| Brake Third (Diag 67) | MRC 9/71 |
| 50' Sleeping Saloon | MRC 9/72 |
| 42' Travelling Post Office | MRC 7/70 |
| 64' Travelling Post Office | MRC 9/72 |
| 6 wheel Parcel Sorting Van | MRC 12/68 |
| 6 wheel Fish Van (Diag 107) | MRY 6/73 |

*Caledonian Railway*

| Item | Reference |
|---|---|
| 45' Non-Corr Composite | MRY 5/75 |
| 45' Non-Corr Third | MRY 5/75 |
| 57' Brake Composite | MRC 1/63 |
| 65' 12 wheel 'Grampian' Stock | MRC 10/60 |
| 4 wheel Carriage Truck (Fish & Game Van) | MRY 1/75 |
| 6 wheel Carriage Truck | RM 11/59 |
| Horse Box (1870) | RM 3/75 |

*Furness Railway*

| Item | Reference |
|---|---|
| 4 wheel Early Carriage | RM 11/66 |
| 6 wheel 31' Brake Third | RM 12/66 |
| 6 wheel Family Saloon | MRY 8/83 |
| 47' Composite (Diag 21) | MRY 4/80 |
| 47' Brake Composite (Diag 22) | MRY 2/80 |
| 48' Third | MRC 3/63 |
|  | RM 12/66 |
| Carriage Truck (1870) | MRY 2/81 |
| Horse Box (1871) | MRY 8/80 |
| Horse Box | RM 1/67 |

*Garstang & Knott End Railway*

| Item | Reference |
|---|---|
| Coach | MRN 10/59 |

*Glasgow & South Western Railway*

| Item | Reference |
|---|---|
| 6 wheel Full Brake | MRC 3/64 |
| 4 wheel Milk and Motor Car Van | MRY 7/75 |
| Director's Saloon No 174 | MRY 2/75 |

*Highland Railway*

| Item | Reference |
|---|---|
| 4 wheel rib-sided Carriage | MRC 6/70 |
| 6 wheel Third (Diag 22) | MRC 12/81 |
| Semi-Corridor Composite | MRC 9/62 |
| 6 wheel Full Brake (Diag 38) | MRC 1/82 |
| Full Brake | MRY 7/73 |
| Director's Saloon No 59 | MRY 6/75 |
| 4 wheel Motor Car Van | RM 1/60 |
| 4 wheel Meat Van | MRC 5/67 |

*Lancashire & Yorkshire Railway*

| Item | Reference |
|---|---|
| Tri-Composite (Diag 26A) | RM 9/78 |
| Tri-Composite (Diag 27A) | RM 9/78 |

**Open Corridor Stock (1900):**

| Item | Reference |
|---|---|
| First | MRC 4/66 |
| Third | MRC 4/66 |
| Brake Composite | MRC 4/66 |

**54' Manchester-Oldham Stock:**

| Item | Reference |
|---|---|
| Composite | RM 7/78 |
| Third | RM 7/78 |
| Brake Third | RM 7/78 |

**54' Corridor Stock:**

| Item | Reference |
|---|---|
| Composite | MRC 7/61 |
| Brake Composite | MRC 7/61 |

**Fireproof Stock (1913):**

| Item | Reference |
|---|---|
| First | RM 1/79 |
| Third | RM 1/79 |
| Brake Third | RM 1/79 |

**Manchester-Bury Electric Stock:**

| Item | Reference |
|---|---|
| Motor Coach | MRC 6/64 |
| Trailer | MRC 6/64 |
| 4 wheel 27'6" Luggage Van | MRY 11/82 |
| 6 wheel Director's Saloon No 1 | MRY 12/75 |
| Superintendant's Saloon No 2 | MRY 12/75 |
| 4 wheel Carriage Truck | RM 4/83 |
| Covered Carriage Truck for Aeroplanes | MRY 12/73 |
| 4 wheel Milk Van | MRC 11/64 |
| 4 wheel Horse Box (Diag 108) | MRY 6/82 |
| 6 wheel Milk Van | MRC 11/64 |

*London & North Western Railway*

| Item | Reference |
|---|---|
| 4 wheel Parliamentary (London & Birmingham Railway) | MRN 6/66 |
| 4 wheel Parliamentary (Manchester & Birmingham Railway) | MRC 9/68 |

**6 wheel 30' Stock:**

| Item | Reference |
|---|---|
| Tri-Composite | MRC 1/69 |
| Third | MRC 11/68 |
| Brake Third | MRC 12/68 |
| Full Brake | MRC 11/68 |
| 42' First | MRC 7/70 |
| 42' Tri-Composite | MRC 6/70 |
| 50' First | MRC 5/71 |
| 50' Third | MRC 10/66 |
| 50' Brake Third | MRC 5/71 |

**50' Arc Roof Corridor Stock:**

| Item | Reference |
|---|---|
| Composite | MRC 6/71 |
| Third | MRC 6/71 |
| Brake Third | MRC 6/71 |

**Cove Roof Corridor Stock:**

| Item | Reference |
|---|---|
| 57' First | MRC 12/71 |
| 57' Composite | MRC 12/71 |
| 57' Third | MRC 12/71 |
| 57' Brake Composite | MRC 12/71 |
| 50' Brake Composite | MRC 12/71 |

**57' Corridor Stock:**

| Item | Reference |
|---|---|
| Composite | MRC 6/72 |
| Third | MRC 6/72 |
| Brake First | MRC 6/72 |
| Brake Composite | MRC 6/72 |
| Brake Third | MRC 6/72 |
| Observation Car | MRC 1/83 |
| Queen Victoria's Day and Night Saloon | RM 1/78 |
| Director's Saloon | MRY 5/74 |
| Director's Saloon No 201 | MRY 8/74 |
| Covered Scenery Truck (Diag 440) | MRY 4/73 |
| Covered Scenery Truck (Diag 442) | MRY 5/73 |
| 6 wheel Parcels Van (Diag 385) | MRY 3/73 |
| 6 wheel Milk Brake Van | MRY 2/73 |
| 6 wheel Fruit Van (Diag 454) | MRY 5/74 |
|  | MRY 8/82 |
| 6 wheel Fish Van | MRY 6/73 |
| 4 wheel Combination Truck (Diag 444) | MRY 8/72 |
| 4 wheel Combination Truck (Diag 444A) | MRY 7/72 |
| 4 wheel Combination Truck (Diag 445) | MRY 12/72 |
|  | MRY 8/82 |
| 4 wheel Combination Truck (Diag 445A) | MRY 1/73 |
|  | MRY 8/82 |
| 4 wheel Covered Truck for Motor Car (Diag 446) | MRY 9/72 |
| 4 wheel Motor Car Truck (Diag 448) | MRY 11/74 |
| 4 wheel Covered Truck for HM Motor Car | MRY 11/72 |
| 4 wheel Chassis non-Passenger Stock | MRN 6/62 |
| 6 wheel Chassis non-Passenger Stock | MRN 6/62 |

*Maryport & Carlisle Railway*

| Item | Reference |
|---|---|
| 6 wheel Composite (1890) | MRY 4/81 |
| 6 wheel 31' Third (Diag 8) | MRY 4/80 |
| 6 wheel Third | MRN 1/67 |
| 4 wheel Brake | MRN 1/67 |
| Horse Box | MRY 2/74 |

*Midland Railway*

| Item | Reference |
|---|---|
| 4 wheel Parliamentary | MRN 2/66 |
| 6 wheel 31' Composite | MRN 3/60 |

**54' Corridor, Clerestory Roof Stock:**

| Item | Reference |
|---|---|
| Composite | MRC 4/68 |
| Third | MRC 6/68 |
| Brake Composite | MRC 5/68 |
| Brake Third | MRC 4/68 |
| Chassis and 8' Bogie | MRC 5/68 |
| Open Third, Clerestory Roof | MRC 10/64 |
| Railmotor No 2234 | MRC 10/74 |
|  | MRC 11/74 |
| Railmotor Trailer No 2235 | MRC 10/74 |
|  | MRC 11/74 |
| Pullman Cars (1874) | MRN 1/59 |
| 6 wheel 31' Full Brake Van | MRY 6/74 |
| 6 wheel Parcel Van | MRY 8/75 |
| 6 wheel Motor Car Van | MRY 6/75 |
| 4 wheel 25' Milk Van | MRY 11/73 |
| 4 wheel Covered Carriage Trunk (Diag 402) | MRY 9/73 |
| 4 wheel Covered Carriage Truck (Diag 403) | MRY 8/73 |

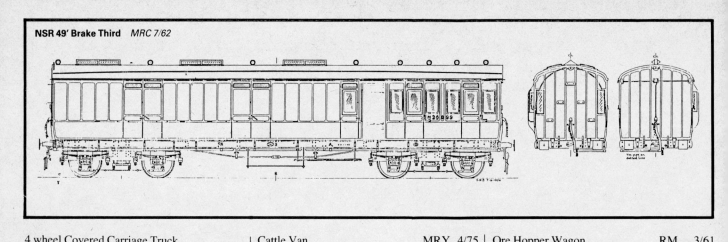

**NSR 49' Brake Third**   *MRC 7/62*

| | | | |
|---|---|---|---|
| 4 wheel Covered Carriage Truck (Diag 406) | MRY 10/73 | | |
| Horse Boxes (Various Diags) | MRY 4/76 | | |

*North London Railway*

| | |
|---|---|
| 4 wheel Coaches | RM 12/71 |
| 4 wheel Full Brake | RM 12/71 |

*North Staffordshire Railway*

| | |
|---|---|
| 49' Brake Third | MRC 7/62 |
| Inspection Saloon No 356 | MRY 1/75 |
| Inspection Saloon – Petrol | MRY 4/75 |
| 4 wheel Milk Van | MRY 1/74 |
| 6 wheel Milk Van | MRY 1/74 |

*Somerset & Dorset Joint Railway*

| | |
|---|---|
| 4 wheel First Nos 1-4 | MRY 6/76 |
| 4 wheel First No 5 | MRY 12/76 |
| 4 wheel Composite (Long Wheelbase) | MRY 8/77 |
| 4 wheel Third | MRY 3/76 |
| 4 wheel Third (Long Wheelbase) | MRY 8/77 |
| 4 wheel Brake Third | MRY 7/76 |
| 4 wheel Full Brake | MRY 8/77 |
| **4 wheel Close Coupled Stock:** | |
|   Second | MRY 7/77 |
|   Third | MRY 7/77 |
|   Brake Third | MRY 7/77 |
| 6 wheel 28'5" Composite | MRY 5/78 |
| **6 wheel 31' Stock:** | |
|   First | MRY 9/78 |
|   Composite | MRY 5/78 |
| | MRC 7/75 |
|   Third | MRY 9/78 |
| | MRC 7/75 |
|   Brake Third | MRY 12/79 |
| | MRY 5/80 |
|   Underframe | MRY 9/78 |
| 47' Composite | MRY 7/80 |
| 46' Composite Luggage | MRY 7/80 |
| 46' Third | MRY 6/84 |
| 46' Brake Third | MRY 11/83 |
| 4 wheel Milk Van | MRY 10/73 |
| 4 wheel 25' Fruit Van | MRY 11/73 |
| 6 wheel 30' Full Brake | MRY 12/79 |
| | MRC 7/75 |
| 32' Underframe | MRY 12/79 |

# Freight Stock

*London Midland & Scottish Railway*

| | |
|---|---|
| 12 ton Covered Goods Van | MRY 1/75 |
| 12 ton Ventilated Van | RM 8/64 |
| | RM 2/67 |
| | MRY 12/73 |
| 12 ton Beer Van | RM 12/63 |
| Banana Van | RM 6/63 |

| | |
|---|---|
| Cattle Van | MRY 4/75 |
| Special Cattle Van | RM 9/69 |
| 20 ton Brake Van (1924) | RM 10/63 |
| 20 ton Brake Van (1933) | RM 7/70 |
| 12 ton Medium Open Wagon | MRY 6/76 |
| 12 ton Low Goods Wagon | RM 3/64 |
| 12 ton Open Wagon (fitted) | RM 9/64 |
| 12 ton Open Wagon | RM 8/66 |
| 12 ton Single Bolster Wagon | RM 5/69 |
| 20 ton Hopper Wagon – Coke | MRY 12/74 |
| 20 ton Loco Coal Wagon | MRY 2/76 |
| 20 ton Long Low Open Wagon | RM 2/64 |
| 20 ton Tube Wagon | RM 7/69 |
| 20 ton Trolley Wagon | MRY 4/77 |
| 30 ton Bogie Bolster Wagon | RM 4/64 |
| Double Bolster Wagon | RM 3/63 |
| 7 plank Mineral Wagon | MRC 6/72 |
| Sand Wagon | RM 5/64 |
| Sleeper Wagon | MRN 7/69 |
| 3 plank Engineer's Wagon | MRN 7/69 |
| FM Container and Chassis | RM 5/70 |
| Open D-Type Container | RM 10/64 |
| Shunter's Truck | MRC 2/63 |

*Caledonian Railway*

| | |
|---|---|
| 6 ton Van | MRN 10/61 |
| | MRN 10/63 |
| 8 ton Refrigerator Van | MRC 2/67 |
| 10 ton Van | MRN 2/63 |
| | MRC 7/64 |
| | MRY 9/82 |
| 6 wheel Brake Van | RM 11/59 |
| Brake Van – Ballast Plow | MRN 11/62 |
| 5 ton Cask Wagon | RM 11/59 |
| 7 ton low-sided Wagon | MRN 5/65 |
| 8 ton low-sided Wagon | MRN 12/65 |
| 8 ton Dropside Wagon | RM 5/74 |
| 10 ton end door Coal Wagon | MRC 6/73 |
| 12 ton Hopper Ballast Wagon | MRN 11/62 |
| 14 ton drop-sided Pig Iron Wagon | RM 7/75 |
| 16 ton end door Coal Wagon | MRN 5/65 |
| 16 ton Tube Wagon | RM 11/59 |
| Machine Wagon | RM 11/59 |

*Furness Railway*

| | |
|---|---|
| Van | RM 1/67 |
| Brake Van | RM 1/67 |
| 6 ton fixed-sided Wagon | MRN 12/66 |
| 6 ton 8 ton Low Sided Wagon | MRN 7/61 |
| 8 ton high-sided Wagon | MRN 7/61 |
| 10 ton low-sided Wagon | MRN 12/66 |
| 10 ton high-sided Wagon | MRN 9/63 |
| 10 ton Open Goods Wagon | RM 1/63 |
| | RM 1/67 |
| Open Wagon | RM 3/61 |
| Dropside Wagon | RM 1/67 |
| Coke Wagon | RM 1/67 |

| | |
|---|---|
| Ore Hopper Wagon | RM 3/61 |
| | RM 1/67 |
| Twin Bolster Wagon | RM 1/67 |

*Glasgow & South Western Railway*

| | |
|---|---|
| 6 ton Van | MRC 7/74 |
| 10 ton Box Van | RM 3/74 |
| 6 ton Cattle Van | MRN 9/62 |
| 8 ton medium sized Wagon | MRC 3/75 |
| 8 ton Open Wagon | MRN 9/65 |
| 8 ton double end door Wagon | MRC 3/71 |
| | MRC 10/82 |
| 8 ton Pig Iron Wagon | RM 9/74 |
| 10 ton drop-sided Wagon | MRN 6/60 |
| 10 ton high-sided Goods Wagon | RM 6/77 |
| 10 ton double end door Wagon | RM 10/79 |
| 10 ton Bolster Wagon | MRY 6/75 |
| 16 ton double door Coal Wagon | RM 7/73 |
| Bar Iron Wagon | RM 1/60 |
| Tube Wagon | RM 1/60 |

*Highland Railway*

| | |
|---|---|
| Double-deck Sheep Van | RM 1/60 |
| | MRC 1/65 |
| Cattle Van | MRN 8/64 |
| 7 ton Timber Wagon | MRC 1/69 |
| 8 ton Open Wagon | MRC 1/69 |
| 8 ton low-sided Open Wagon | MRN 1/62 |
| 8 ton low-sided Open Wagon | MRN 4/62 |
| 8 ton medium-sided Open Wagon | MRN 1/62 |
| 8 ton Coal Wagon | MRN 5/62 |

*Lancashire & Yorkshire Railway*

| | |
|---|---|
| 10 ton Van | MRN 11/69 |
| | RM 8/72 |
| 10 ton Van (fitted) | RM 2/78 |
| 10 ton Covered Van | RM 7/72 |
| 10 ton Fish Van (fitted) | RM 6/78 |
| 12 ton Goods Van | MRC 3/70 |
| 12 ton Goods Van (fitted) | MRC 2/70 |
| Fish Van | MRN 6/71 |
| Cattle Van | RM 8/72 |
| Insulated & Refrigerated Vans | MRC 6/66 |
| 10 ton Brake Vans | MRN 10/70 |
| | RM 12/72 |
| 20 ton 6 wheel Brake Van | RM 5/72 |
| 10 ton drop-side Wagon | MRN 6/69 |
| 12 ton Coal Wagon | RM 4/72 |
| 12 ton double end door Coal Wagon | MRC 1/83 |
| 12 ton Single Bolster Timber Wagon | RM 2/81 |
| 15 ton 6 wheel Deal Wagon | MRN 12/64 |
| 20 ton Mineral Wagon | MRN 3/64 |
| | RM 6/64 |
| 20 ton double end door Coal Wagon (fitted) | RM 2/74 |

Low-sided Goods Wagon RM 11/79
3 plank drop-side Wagon MRN 2/62
Low Goods Wagon RM 8/63
6 wheel Flat Wagon MRN 6/70
Piece Wagon RM 11/79

*London & North Western Railway*
6 ton Van MRN 6/63
6 ton Van (fitted) MRN 4/61
6 ton Cattle Van MRN 1/64
10 ton Vans MRC 2/65
10 ton Van (fitted) MRN 2/65
10 ton Malt/Ale Van MRN 7/66
10 ton Gunpowder Van MRN 6/63
Cattle Van with Compartment MRY 4/74
Van (1851) MRY 4/78
20 ton Brake Van MRN 11/60
20 ton 6 wheel Brake Van MRC 1/72
6 ton high-sided Wagon RM 6/73
6 ton drop-sided Ballast Wagon RM 9/77
10 ton high-sided Goods Wagon RM 2/77
10 ton low-sided Wagon RM 5/77
10 ton Loco Coal Wagon RM 2/63
10 ton Slate Truck MRY 2/82
30 ton Timber Trolley MRY 4/73
Twin Match Trucks MRN 2/64

*London, Tilbury & Southend Railway*
10 ton Goods Van RM 11/79
Cattle Van MRC 6/71
Brake Van – Birdcage MRY 4/75
Brake Van – Rebuilt without
  Birdcage MRY 4/75
10 ton Single Bolster Timber
  Wagon MRN 3/61

*Maryport & Carlisle Railway*
8 ton Van MRC 7/65
9 ton low-sided Wagon MRN 10/60
10 ton low-sided Wagon MRN 2/61

*Midland Railway*
8 ton Van MRN 5/64
   RM 6/83
8 ton Banana Van (fitted) RM 6/76
   RM 11/78
10 ton Goods Van RM 9/79
Box Van – Outside Braced RM 6/72
Meat Van MRN 5/61
Refrigerator Meat Van (fitted) RM 12/75
   RM 3/76
   RM 2/79

Banana Van MRN 6/61
Cattle Van RM 1/77
Long Cattle Van RM 6/74
6 wheel Fish Van RM 4/67
10 ton Brake Van – Tariff Van MRN 7/65
15/20 ton 6 wheel Brake Van MRN 2/60
Brake Van (1870) MRN 6/60
Brake Van MRN 11/61
6 ton Open Wagon (fitted) RM 10/73
8 ton Goods and Mineral Wagon RM 8/74
8 ton low-sided Wagon MRN 9/61
8/10 ton low-sided Open Wagon MRN 11/61
8 ton high-sided Goods and
  Mineral Wagon MRN 3/67
8 ton Coke Wagon MRN 6/69
8 ton Hopper Wagon MRN 12/63
8 ton low drop-sided Ballast
  Wagon RM 4/79
10 ton low-sided Open Wagon MRN 12/65
10 ton Single Bolster Timber
  Wagon MRN 3/61
12 ton high-sided Goods and
  Mineral Wagon (EKD) RM 10/74
12 ton high-sided Goods and
  Mineral Wagon RM 5/75
12 ton high-sided Wagon RM 1/75
20 ton Flat Wagon MRY 4/74
5 plank Open Wagon MRN 6/65
   MRY 9/73
   MRY 4/74
   RM 7/80
Ballast Wagon RM 9/83
Sleeper Wagon MRN 5/66
5 ton Travelling Crane MRN 8/66

*North London Railway*
9 ton Hopper Coal Wagon MRY 10/71

*North Staffordshire Railway*
8 ton Goods Van RM 11/75
8 ton low-sided Wagon MRN 8/63
10 ton end door Coal Wagon MRC 10/69
Single Bolster Wagon MRN 9/65

*Somerset & Dorset Joint Railway*
8 ton Goods Van (LSWR
  Design) RM 4/79
8 ton Road Van MRC 9/65
8 ton low-sided Goods Wagon RM 7/74
5 plank Open Wagon MRN 6/65

*Stratford-upon-Avon & Midland Junction
  Railway*
8 ton Van (fitted) MRN 8/61
10 ton low-sided Open Wagon MRN 8/61

# Structures

*London, Midland & Scottish Railway*
Goods Shed – Prefabricated MRY 10/75
Warehouse MRY 10/73
Signalbox – E Division, Timber MRY 6/73
Signalbox – All Wood MRY 10/74
Signalbox – Nameboard MRY 9/74
Signalbox – Coal Bunker &
  Toilets MRY 2/75
Station Roof Barge Board MRN 2/62
Station Seat MRY 11/76
Station Indicator Board MRY 6/78
Station Nameboard MRN 11/70
   MRY 1/75
Station Timetable/Poster Board MRC 11/70
Platform Trolleys MRY 7/75
Chalkboard MRY 9/77
Station Lamp MRY 6/75
Canteen – Chaddesden MRC 8/81
Coal Shed MRY 10/84
Platelayers Hut MRY 7/76
Lineside Hut MRC 9/82
Cycle Shed MRY 4/76
Chemical Convenience Hut MRY 6/76
Lamp Hut MRY 2/77
Warning Sign MRY 2/76
Lamp Posts – Reinforced
  Concrete MRY 3/76
Fire Bucket Box MRY 4/76
Bins – Concrete MRY 4/77
Sandbox – Concrete MRY 5/77
Stiles and V-Gates MRY 8/76
Level Crossing/Gate Machine MRY 6/77
Milepost MRY 3/77
Gradient Post MRY 3/78
Loading Gauge MRY 5/78
TPO Lineside Apparatus MRY 11/77
**Signals:**
  Single Post Signals MRN 3/71
  Signal Arms MRC 11/70
   MRN 2/71
  Spectacle Plates and Backlight
   Binders MRC 3/71
  Lattice Posts MRC 12/70
   MRN 3/71
  Wood Posts MRN 3/71

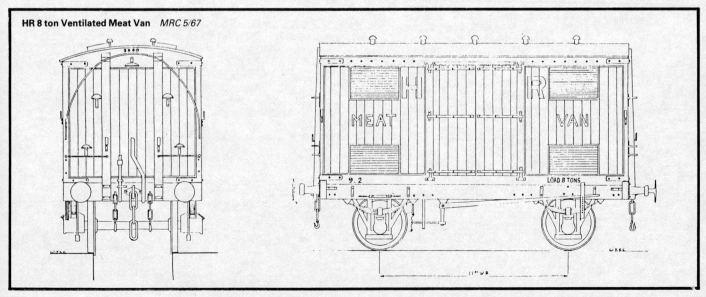

**HR 8 ton Ventilated Meat Van** *MRC 5/67*

| 1-Doll Half Bracket | MRN 6/71 |
| 2-Doll Bracket | MRN 7/71 |
| 2-Doll Broad Flange Beam Bracket | MRC 6/71 |
| 2-Doll Bracket on Lattice Post | MRC 1/71 |
| 2-Doll Bracket with Elevated Balance Levers | MRC 8/71 |
| | MRN 8/71 |
| 3-Doll Bracket | RM 5/81 |
| 3-Doll Bracket on Lattice Post | MRC 7/71 |
| Tubular Steel Post | MRN 3/71 |
| | MRC 5/71 |
| Ladder | MRN 5/63 |
| Ladder Bow | MRN 7/63 |
| Banner Repeaters | MRN 5/71 |
| Shunt Limit Indicator | MRC 10/70 |
| Sight Boards | MRN 4/71 |
| Single Post Colour Light | MRC 10/72 |
| Gantry Colour Light | MRC 11/72 |
| Position Colour Light and Junction | MRC 12/72 |
| Ground | MRC 1/85 |
| Summary | MRC 3/84 |

### Caledonian Railway
**Stations:**
| Longforgan | MRY 3/75 |
| Lesmahagow | RM 4/70 |
| Errol | RM 4/70 |
| | RM 5/70 |
| Station Footbridge | RM 5/70 |
| Station Valance | MRN 9/60 |

**Signalboxes:**
| Dubton | RM 4/70 |
| Kelvinbridge | RM 9/64 |
| Kirtlebridge | MRN 12/67 |
| Lesmahagow Junction | MRC 6/72 |
| Polmadie | RM 3/70 |
| Goods Shed – Timber | RM 5/70 |
| Bowstring Girder Bridge | RM 3/71 |
| Milepost | RM 5/70 |
| Signals | MRN 5/63 |
| | MRC 1/69 |
| | RM 3/71 |
| Lattice Signal Posts | MRN 2/63 |
| Signals – Ground | RM 3/70 |
| | MRC 1/85 |
| Signals Summary | MRC 8/84 |

**LMSR Standard 2-Doll Bracket Signal** *MRC 1/71*

### Cockermouth, Keswick & Penrith Railway
| Threlkeld Station | MRC 7/77 |

### Furness Railway
**Stations:**
| Arkholme (FR and MR Joint) | MRY 8/75 |
| Barrow Central | RM 5/66 |
| Borwick (FR and MR Joint) | MRY 8/75 |
| Carnforth (FR and MR Joint) | RM 3/67 |
| Greenodd | RM 2/62 |
| Haverthwaite | MRC 4/73 |
| Windermere Lakeside | RM 5/65 |

**Signalboxes:**
| Greenodd | RM 2/62 |
| Kent's Bank | RM 2/62 |
| Leven | RM 2/62 |
| Windermere Lakeside | RM 5/65 |
| Goods Shed – Greenodd | RM 2/62 |
| Water Column | RM 11/62 |
| Signal | RM 2/62 |
| Signal Cap | MRN 9/63 |
| Signals – Ground | MRC 1/85 |
| Signals Summary | MRC 3/84 |

### Glasgow & South Western Railway
| Barassie Station | RM 3/75 |
| Surfacemen's Cottages | RM 3/76 |
| Signals | MRN 5/63 |
| | MRC 1/69 |
| Signals – Ground | MRC 1/85 |
| Signals Summary | MRC 8/84 |

### Highland Railway
**Stations:**
| Carrbridge | RM 3/76 |
| Duirnish | RM 3/76 |
| Newtonmore | RM 4/76 |
| Plockton | RM 4/76 |
| Station Nameboard | RM 7/66 |
| Loco Shed – Kyle of Lochalsh | RM 11/73 |
| Viaduct – Calvine | MRC 10/84 |
| Stone Arch Bridge | MRC 7/70 |
| Water Tank | RM 5/75 |
| Signals | MRN 5/63 |
| | MRC 11/68 |
| Signal Finial | MRN 8/62 |
| Signal – Ground | MRC 1/85 |
| Signals Summary | MRC 8/84 |

### Lancashire & Yorkshire Railway
**Stations:**
| Brierfield | MRC 11/75 |
| Lightcliffe | MRN 8/69 |
| Rishworth | MRC 8/68 |
| Platform Waiting Room | MRY 10/73 |
| Station Nameboard | MRY 1/75 |
| Messrooms | MRN 11/69 |
| Signalbox – Clayton West | MRN 2/70 |
| Signalbox – Dewsbury East Jcn | RM 6/64 |
| Signalbox Nameboard | RM 12/72 |
| Goods Shed – Liversedge | MRN 9/69 |
| Goods Shed – Rishworth | MRC 8/68 |
| Loco Shed – 4 Road | MRN 2/70 |
| Coaling Stage | MRN 1/70 |
| | RM 12/83 |
| Cattle Dock | MRN 11/69 |
| Coal Staiths | RM 12/83 |
| Water Tank | MRN 11/69 |
| Signal – Ground | MRC 1/85 |
| Signal Landings and Galleries | MRN 8/63 |
| Signal Ladder | MRN 5/63 |
| Signal Finial | MRN 9/62 |
| Signals Summary | MRC 3/84 |

| | |
|---|---|
| Mileposts | MRY 3/77 |
| Gradient Posts | MRY 3/78 |

*Lancashire Union & Joint Railway*

| | |
|---|---|
| Goods Shed – Feniscowles | MRC 7/71 |

*London & North Western Railway*
**Stations:**

| | |
|---|---|
| Donnington | MRC 6/68 |
| St Albans | RM 7/84 |
| Hadlow (LNWR/GWR Joint) | RM 2/80 |
| Wooden Built | RM 12/62 |
| Station Valance | MRN 9/60 |
| | MRN 2/62 |
| Station Screen | MRN 3/60 |
| Station Lamps | RM 12/62 |
| Station Indicator Boards | MRY 6/78 |
| Platform Seat | MRY 11/76 |
| Platform Trolley | MRY 7/75 |
| Lamp Hut | MRY 2/77 |

**Signalboxes:**

| | |
|---|---|
| Burton & Holme No 2 | RM 4/69 |
| | RM 9/74 |
| Kenilworth Jcn | MRY 7/74 |
| Warrington, Arpley Jcn | RM 4/84 |
| Northampton – Market Harborough | RM 4/85 |
| Standard Type | RM 4/69 |
| | MRC 12/70 |
| | RM 9/74 |
| Window Frames | MRC 4/73 |
| Weighbridge Offices | MRY 12/76 |
| Stables | MRY 1/76 |
| Loco Shed | RM 3/68 |
| | MRC 3/77 |
| Coaling Stage | MRC 9/76 |
| 60' Turntable | RM 1/73 |
| Bridge – Edgeware St Liverpool | RM 7/71 |
| Canal Bridge – Patricroft | MRC 12/82 |
| Viaduct – Widnes | RM 10/73 |
| Water Column | MRC 12/74 |
| Water Tank | MRC 4/75 |
| Fencing | MRY 12/77 |
| V-Gates and Stiles | MRY 8/76 |
| Siding Gates | MRY 10/77 |
| Loading Gauge | MRY 5/78 |
| Buffer Stop | RM 7/83 |
| Milepost | MRN 7/59 |
| Gradient Post | MRN 11/63 |
| | MRY 3/78 |
| Signals | MRN 5/63 |
| | RM 3/65 |
| | RM 4/68 |
| | MRN 7/68 |
| | MRC 2/69 |
| | RM 7/83 |
| | MRC 3/84 |

*London, Tilbury & Southend Railway*

| | |
|---|---|
| Platform Seat | MRC 10/66 |
| Signal – Ground | MRC 1/85 |
| Signals Summary | MRC 3/84 |

*Maryport & Carlisle Railway*

| | |
|---|---|
| Loco Shed – Castle Currock | MRY 8/78 |
| Signal Ladder | MRN 5/63 |

*Midland Railway*
**Stations:**

| | |
|---|---|
| Bakewell | RM 12/74 |
| Bamford | MRY 1/77 |
| Clapham | RM 1/65 |
| Dudbridge | MRY 3/85 |
| Elstree | MRC 7/64 |
| Hawes | MRC 5/78 |
| Haworth | MRN 5/66 |
| Nailsworth | MRY 9/79 |
| Northampton St Johns | MRC 5/80 |
| Oakworth | MRN 12/66 |
| Oxenhope | MRN 11/66 |
| Rowsley | MRC 11/73 |
| Saltaire | MRN 2/66 |
| Typical | MRC 11/62 |
| Typical Settle & Carlisle | RM 11/63 |
| Station Waiting Room – Duffield | RM 11/82 |
| Station Waiting Shelter | MRY 1/77 |
| Station Footbridge | MRC 7/64 |
| | RM 7/67 |
| | RM 2/75 |
| | MRY 6/75 |
| | RM 5/83 |
| Station Nameboard | MRN 4/65 |
| | RM 6/71 |
| | RM 3/75 |
| Station Decorative Awning Bracket | MRC 11/62 |
| Station Drinking Water Fountain | MRY 12/74 |
| Platform Indicator Post | MRY 11/74 |
| Platform Seat | MRC 11/62 |
| | MRC 10/66 |
| Platform Barrows and Trolleys | MRC 11/62 |
| | MRY 4/75 |
| Platform Food Trolley | MRY 4/75 |
| Platform Lighting Trolley | MRY 7/75 |
| Platform Fire Bucket Box | MRY 4/76 |

**Signalboxes:**

| | |
|---|---|
| Bakewell | RM 3/75 |
| Clapham | RM 1/65 |
| Gloucester Barnwood | MRN 7/62 |
| Northampton St Johns | MRC 7/80 |
| Standard | MRN 6/60 |
| Basic Types | MRC 4/82 |
| Signalbox Coal Bunker | MRY 2/75 |
| Lever Frame | MRN 1/64 |
| Ground Frame | MRN 7/62 |

**Goods Shed:**

| | |
|---|---|
| Bakewell | RM 11/74 |
| Hawes | MRC 6/78 |
| Settle & Carlisle | RM 11/63 |
| Typical | RM 4/78 |
| Warehouse | RM 9/81 |
| Carriage Shed | MRC 8/80 |
| Coal Depot Office | MRN 10/63 |
| | RM 1/75 |
| Weighbridge | RM 6/75 |
| | MRC 5/78 |
| Offices – Northampton | MRC 5/80 |
| | MRC 6/80 |
| | MRC 7/80 |

**Loco Sheds:**

| | |
|---|---|
| Coalville | MRN 1/65 |
| Hellifield | RM 11/63 |
| Rowsley | RM 4/80 |
| Typical 2-road | RM 8/81 |
| Coaling Stage | RM 1/69 |
| | MRC 9/70 |
| | RM 12/73 |
| 53' Turntable | MRN 5/60 |
| Sandhouse | MRN 1/65 |
| Platelayer's Hut | MRN 1/60 |
| | MRY 10/78 |
| Lamp Hut | MRY 2/77 |
| Toilet – Wooden | MRY 2/75 |
| Overbridge | RM 3/75 |
| | MRC 4/78 |
| Girder Bridge | MRC 10/81 |
| Viaduct – Hawes | MRC 4/78 |
| Bridge Number Plates | MRY 6/75 |
| Water Tower | RM 11/63 |
| | RM 12/73 |
| Water Column | RM 1/65 |
| | MRC 11/65 |
| Buffer Stops | MRC 9/65 |
| Level Crossing Gates | MRY 6/77 |
| V-Gates and Stiles | MRY 8/76 |
| Loading Gauge | MRN 2/61 |
| | MRY 8/73 |
| | MRY 5/78 |
| Mileposts | MRY 3/77 |
| Gradient Posts | MRY 3/78 |

**Signals:**

| | |
|---|---|
| Single Post | MRC 12/61 |
| | RM 6/71 |
| Bracket | MRC 12/61 |
| | RM 1/65 |
| | RM 7/71 |
| Gantry | RM 8/71 |
| Stop and Shunt | RM 9/71 |
| Gallows and Tunnel | RM 12/71 |
| Arms | RM 6/71 |
| Landings and Galleries | MRN 8/63 |
| Ladder | MRN 5/63 |
| Ground Disc | RM 10/71 |
| | MRC 1/85 |
| Summary | MRC 3/84 |

*North Staffordshire Railway*

| | |
|---|---|
| Station Nameboard | RM 9/72 |
| Station Bargeboard | MRN 2/62 |
| Level Crossing | MRY 7/77 |
| Signal Ladder | MRN 5/63 |
| Signal Finial | MRN 8/62 |
| Signal – Ground | MRC 1/85 |
| Signals Summary | MRC 3/84 |

*Portpatrick & Wigtownshire Joint Railway*

| | |
|---|---|
| Castle Kennedy Station | RM 12/77 |

*Stratford-upon-Avon & Midland Junction Railway*
**Stations:**

| | |
|---|---|
| Binton | MRY 5/79 |
| Blakesley | RM 3/68 |
| Ettington | MRN 1/64 |
| Signalbox – Ettington | MRN 1/64 |
| Goods Shed – Ettington | MRN 1/64 |

*Somerset & Dorset Joint Railway*

| | |
|---|---|
| Bridgwater Station | RM 3/61 |
| Burnham-on-Sea Station | RM 1/63 |
| Signalbox – Burnham-on-Sea | RM 1/63 |
| Signalbox – Midsomer Norton | RM 12/84 |
| Goods Shed – Burnham-on-Sea | RM 1/63 |
| Stores/Offices – Templecombe | RM 5/61 |
| Store – Radstock | MRY 10/72 |
| Signals – Summary | MRC 10/83 |

*Wirral Railway*

| | |
|---|---|
| Goods Shed – New Brighton | MRC 12/69 |

# Track Plans

| | |
|---|---|
| Aber (LNWR) | RM 7/75 |
| Abergele and Pensarn (LNWR) | RM 10/75 |
| Alfreton and South Normanton (MR) | MRC 10/83 |
| Amlwch (LNWR) | RM 6/75 |
| | MRY 6/82 |
| Apperley Jcn (MR) | RM 11/71 |
| Arkholme (FR/MR) | MRY 8/75 |
| Armathwaite (MR) | MRC 10/83 |
| Arnside (FR) | MRC 10/65 |

| Location | Drawing | Date |
|---|---|---|
| Aviemore Loco Shed (HR) | MRN | 2/66 |
| Bakewell (MR) | RM | 4/63 |
| Ballachulish (CR) | RM | 4/76 |
| Baildon (MR) | MRN | 12/70 |
| Banbury (LNWR) | RM | 4/62 |
| Bassenthwaite Lake (CKPR) | MRC | 4/77 |
| Bath Green Park (SDJR) | RM | 12/80 |
| Battyford (LNWR) | MRN | 8/70 |
| | MRC | 1/72 |
| Beeston (MR) | MRC | 7/80 |
| Bedford (BR) | RM | 3/79 |
| Bettws-y-Coed (LNWR) | RM | 9/75 |
| | MRY | 10/81 |
| Billing (LNWR) | MRN | 3/71 |
| Blaenau Ffestiniog (LNWR) | RM | 11/62 |
| | MRY | 11/81 |
| Blencow (CKPR) | RM | 8/63 |
| Bolsover (MR) | RM | 1/82 |
| Bolton Abbey (MR) | MRN | 12/70 |
| Borrowash (MR) | MRC | 10/83 |
| Borwick (FR/MR) | MRY | 8/75 |
| Bricket Wood (LNWR) | RM | 2/85 |
| Brierfield (LYR) | MRC | 11/75 |
| Buxton LNWR Loco Shed | MRC | 1/82 |
| Buxton MR Loco Shed | MRC | 1/82 |
| Buxworth Jcn (MR) | RM | 8/73 |
| Caernarvon (LNWR) | MRY | 7/82 |
| Carnforth Loco Shed (Preservation) | RM | 8/78 |
| Castle Kennedy (PWR) | RM | 12/77 |
| Cheadle (NSR) | RM | 3/62 |
| Chesterfield (MR) | MRC | 10/83 |
| Chinley (MR) | MRC | 10/83 |
| Clayton West (LYR) | MRC | 4/74 |
| | MRY | 9/77 |
| Clayton West Jcn | MRY | 10/77 |
| Cleckheaton (LYR) | MRY | 7/78 |
| Coaley Jcn (MR) | RM | 7/69 |
| Coniston (FR) | RM | 9/62 |
| Conway (LNWR) | MRY | 12/81 |
| Daventry (LNWR) | RM | 1/64 |
| Deganwy (LNWR) | RM | 8/75 |
| Denbigh (LNWR) | MRY | 4/81 |
| Dent (MR) | RM | 2/61 |
| Derby (MR) | MRC | 9/78 |
| Devons Road Diesel Depot (BR) | RM | 4/59 |
| Didsbury (MR) | RM | 2/83 |
| Donnington (LNWR) | MRC | 6/68 |
| Dornoch (HR) | RM | 3/73 |
| Duffield (MR) | RM | 11/83 |
| Ettington (SMJR) | MRN | 1/64 |
| Evercreech Jcn (SDJR) | RM | 7/84 |
| Fenny Stratford (LNWR) | RM | 9/63 |
| Fort George (HR) | MRY | 1/75 |
| Fortrose (HR) | RM | 3/73 |
| | MRY | 3/76 |
| Foxfield (FR) | RM | 9/62 |
| Garsdale (MR) | RM | 2/66 |
| Gaerwen (LNWR) | MRY | 6/82 |
| Govilon (LNWR) | RM | 3/76 |
| Gowhole Sidings (MR) | RM | 8/73 |
| Grayrigg (LNWR) | RM | 2/75 |
| Greenodd (FR) | RM | 2/62 |
| Haigh (LYR) | MRY | 9/78 |
| Hanley (NSR) | MRY | 2/78 |
| Harbourne (LNWR) | RM | 10/62 |
| Harrington (LNWR) | RM | 1/76 |
| Hasland Loco Shed (MR) | MRC | 6/80 |
| Hawes (MR) | RM | 4/76 |
| Hayfield (MR/GCR) | RM | 8/73 |
| Hebden Bridge (LYR) | MRC | 1/72 |
| | MRY | 1/75 |
| Hellifield (MR) | MRC | 6/76 |
| Helmsdale (HR) | RM | 3/73 |
| Highbridge Loco Shed (SDJR) | MRN | 5/66 |
| Hinckley (LNWR) | RM | 5/64 |
| Holmfirth (LYR) | MRN | 5/69 |
| | MRY | 12/77 |
| | MRC | 6/77 |
| Holywell Town (LNWR) | RM | 5/62 |
| Inverness (HR) | MRC | 5/75 |
| Kenilworth Jcn (LNWR) | MRY | 7/74 |
| | MRY | 10/77 |
| Kenyon Jcn (LNWR) | RM | 2/82 |
| Kettering Loco Shed (MR) | MRN | 10/66 |
| Killin (CR) | MRN | 3/63 |
| Kirkby Lonsdale (LNWR) | RM | 7/74 |
| | RM | 11/74 |
| Kirkby Stephen (MR) | RM | 2/61 |
| Kyle of Lochalsh (HR) | MRN | 12/65 |
| | MRC | 5/75 |
| Kyle of Lochalsh Loco Shed (HR) | RM | 3/75 |
| Langwathby (MR) | RM | 2/61 |
| Lightcliffe (LYR) | MRN | 7/70 |
| Liversedge (LYR) | MRN | 7/70 |
| | MRY | 8/78 |
| Llanberis (LNWR) | MRC | 6/74 |
| | MRY | 7/82 |
| Llangefni (LNWR) | RM | 7/63 |
| | RM | 11/75 |
| Llangunllo (LNWR) | RM | 12/75 |
| Llanrwst (LNWR) | MRY | 8/81 |
| Loch Tay (CR) | MRN | 3/63 |
| Longforgen (CR) | MRY | 1/75 |
| Low Gill (LNWR) | RM | 1/75 |
| Lybster (HR) | RM | 3/73 |
| Lymm (LNWR) | RM | 11/74 |
| Macclesfield (LNWR) | RM | 7/64 |
| Mansfield Loco Shed (MR) | MRC | 6/80 |
| Market Harborough (MR/LNWR) | MRN | 9/65 |
| Marsden (LNWR) | MRN | 8/70 |
| Melling (FR/MR) | MRY | 8/75 |
| Menai Bridge (LNWR) | RM | 2/76 |
| | MRY | 2/82 |
| Millers Dale (MR) | RM | 5/83 |
| Mirfield Loco Shed (LYR) | MRN | 12/69 |
| Mold (LNWR) | MRY | 3/81 |
| | MRY | 2/83 |
| Mossley Hill (LNWR) | RM | 12/62 |
| Muir of Ord (HR) | RM | 3/73 |
| Nailsworth (MR) | MRY | 9/79 |
| New Mills Jcn (MR) | RM | 8/73 |
| New Mills South Jcn (MR) | RM | 8/73 |
| Northampton St Johns (MR) | MRC | 5/80 |
| Oban (CR) | MRY | 1/74 |
| Over and Wharton (LNWR) | RM | 6/62 |
| Penmaenmawr (LNWR) | MRY | 1/82 |
| Pellon (LYR) | MRY | 4/78 |
| Poulton-le-Fylde (LNWR/LYR) | MRC | 8/77 |
| Ravensthorpe (LNWR) | MRC | 1/72 |
| Ribblehead (MR) | MRC | 5/77 |
| Rickmansworth (LNWR) | RM | 5/75 |
| Ruthin (LNWR) | RM | 12/63 |
| | MRY | 5/81 |
| St Albans — Abbey (LNWR) | RM | 3/63 |
| | RM | 7/83 |
| | RM | 7/84 |
| St Albans Loco Shed (MR) | MRN | 3/66 |
| Settle (MR) | RM | 2/66 |
| Shap (LNWR) | RM | 4/75 |
| Shap Summit Sidings (LNWR) | RM | 4/75 |
| Shepley (LYR) | MRY | 11/77 |
| Shirebrook West (MR) | MRC | 10/83 |
| Southport, Lord St (LYR) | MRN | 2/59 |
| Sowerby Bridge Loco Shed (LYR) | MRY | 2/78 |
| Spondon (MR) | MRC | 9/80 |
| Stanbridgeford (LNWR) | RM | 10/74 |
| Stanley Jcn (CR/HR) | MRN | 9/62 |
| Stirling (BR) | RM | 5/79 |
| Strathpeffer (HR) | RM | 3/73 |
| Tain (HR) | RM | 3/73 |
| Talacre (LNWR) | RM | 9/74 |
| Tewkesbury (MR) | MRN | 3/71 |
| Thelwall (LNWR) | RM | 2/64 |
| The Mound (HR) | RM | 3/73 |
| Thongs Bridge (LYR) | MRY | 1/78 |
| Threlkeld (CKPR) | MRC | 7/77 |
| Towcester (SMJR) | MRY | 12/76 |
| Trent (MR) | MRC | 10/83 |
| Thurso (HR) | RM | 3/73 |
| | MRC | 5/75 |
| Wellingborough (MR) | MRN | 3/71 |
| Westhouses Loco Shed (MR) | MRC | 6/80 |
| Wick (HR) | MRC | 5/75 |
| Wick Loco Shed (HR) | MRN | 2/67 |
| Wigton (MCR) | MRC | 1/78 |
| Windermere (FR) | MRC | 11/66 |
| | MRC | 2/81 |
| Wirksworth (MR) | RM | 11/83 |

Left: The unique Midland Railway 0-10-0 Lickey Incline banking locomotive 'Big Bertha' in final condition as British Railways No 58100. (Drawings RM 10/67 and 11/67). _D. Penney_

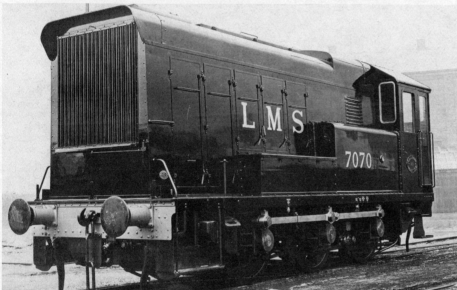

*Above:* **LMS 'Royal Scot' Lounge First Brake No 15493 as built. (Drawing RM 11/67).**
*Real Photographs (3404)*

*Left:* **LMS 350hp English Electric 0-6-0 diesel shunter No 7070 built by Hawthorn Leslie 1936. (Drawing MRY 8/75).**
*Locomotive Publishing Co (9291)*

*Below left:* **View of Wirksworth goods yard from station looking towards Duffield on 5 August 1952. (Track plan RM 11/83).** *R. H. Hughes*

# London & North Eastern Railway

## Locomotives

**4-2-2**
Class X4 (ex-GCR) — MRN 7/67

**0-4-0**
Class Y10 (ex-NBR) — RM 10/66

**2-4-0**
Class E4 (ex-GER) — MRY 2/84
Class E6 (ex-NER) — RM 9/75
— MRY 1/77

**4-4-0**
Class D2 (ex-GNR) — RM 12/72
— MRY 11/84
Class D9 (ex-GCR) — MRN 9/63
Class D10 (ex-GCR) — RM 9/68
Class D11 (ex-GCR) — MRC 1/62
— RM 8/69
— MRY 5/74
Class D11 chimneys — MRC 2/75
Class D19 (ex-NER) — MRC 3/60
Class D31 (ex-NBR) — RM 2/66
Class D34 (ex-NBR) — RM 12/68
Class D40 (ex-GNSR) — MRN 7/61
Class D41 (ex-GNSR) — MRN 4/63
Class D49 — RM 10/66
Class D50 (ex-NBR) — MRN 1/62

**4-4-2**
Class C1 (ex-GNR) — MRC 5/60
Class C2 (ex-GNR) — RM 2/75
Class C11 (ex-NBR) — RM 3/76

**0-6-0**
Class J6 (ex-GNR) — RM 8/66
Class J11 (ex-GCR) — MRN 7/62
— MRC 1/70
Class J27 (ex-NER) — RM 6/66
Class J28 (ex-HBR) — RM 9/76
Class J35 (ex-NBR) — RM 3/68
Class J37 (ex-NBR) — MRN 8/62
— MRY 3/72
— RM 5/68
Class J40 (ex-M&GN) — MRN 10/63

**2-6-0**
Class K2 (ex-GNR) — MRY 3/75

**2-6-2**
Class V2 — MRN 4/66

**4-6-0**
Class B1 — MRY 11/76
Class B3 (ex-GCR) — RM 10/72
Class B4 (ex-GCR) — MRC 9/63
Class B5 (ex-GCR) — MRN 1/64
Class B12/3 — RM 11/72
— RM 4/73
Class B17 — MRC 2/59

**4-6-2**
Class A1 (ex-GNR) — MRN 8/60
— MRY 4/72
Class A2 (ex-NER) — RM 1/85
Class A2 — RM 1/70
Class A3 — RM 8/60
— RM 12/72
— RM 6/83
Class A4 — RM 9/71
— MRY 7/76
— MRC 3/75
— MRC 5/75
— MRC 8/75

**0-8-0**
Class Q4 (ex-GCR) — MRN 2/63
Class Q5 (ex-NER) — MRN 12/65
Class Q10 (ex-HBR) — RM 3/79

**2-8-0**
Class 01 (ex-GNR) — RM 8/72
Class 02 (ex-GNR) — RM 8/72
Class 04 (ex-GCR) — MRN 11/61
— RM 10/65

**4-4-2T**
Class C12 (ex-GNR) — MRC 8/71
Class C13 (ex-GCR) — RM 6/67
— RM 11/68
Class C14 (ex-GCR) — RM 6/67
Class C17 (ex-M&GN) — MRC 2/60

**4-4-4T**
Class H2 (ex-Met R) — MRC 6/61

**0-6-0T**
Class J50 (ex-GNR) — MRN 2/69
Class J58 (ex-GCR) — MRC 12/68
Class J59 (ex-GCR) — MRC 12/68
Class J67 (ex-GER) — MRY 1/84
Class J69 (ex-GER) — MRY 3/72
— MRY 11/82
Class J83 (ex-NBR) — MRN 2/65
Class J93 (ex-M&GN) — MRC 4/71

**0-6-0ST**
Class J52 (ex-GNR) — MRN 4/65
Class J94 — RM 10/73

**0-6-2T**
Class N2 (ex-GNR) — RM 4/77
— RM 9/82
Class N4 (ex-GCR) — RM 11/70
Class N5 (ex-GCR) — RM 11/70
Class N8 (ex-NER) — RM 7/71
Class N9 (ex-NER) — RM 7/71
Class N10 (ex-NER) — RM 7/71

Class N15 (ex-NBR) — MRN 2/64
— RM 9/67
Class N18 (ex-CVHR) — MRC 3/62

**0-6-4T**
Class M1 (ex-GCR) — RM 4/78
Class M2 (ex-Met R) — MRC 1/72

**2-8-2**
Class P1 — RM 1/73
Class P2 — RM 3/73
Class P2 (semi-streamlined) — RM 3/73

**0-4-0T**
Class Y1 — MRC 5/64
Class Y3 — MRC 5/64
Class Y6 (ex-GER) — RM 7/61
— MRY 3/84
Class Y7 (ex-NER) — RM 7/72
Class Y8 (ex-NER) — MRC 11/59
— MRN 1/69
— RM 7/72

**0-4-0ST**
Class Y5 (ex-GER) — MRY 8/72
Class Y9 (ex-NBR) — MRN 10/67

**0-4-2T**
Class Z5 (ex-GNSR) — MRC 7/68

**0-4-4T**
Class G3 (ex-GCR) — MRC 3/76
— MRC 8/76
Class G5 (ex-NER) — MRC 9/60
Class G6 (ex-NER) — MRY 7/79

**2-4-2T**
Class F1 (ex-GCR) — RM 11/67
Class F4 (ex-GER) — MRY 3/76
Class F8 (ex-NER) — RM 9/72

**4-4-0T**
Class D51 (ex-NBR) — MRC 3/77

**2-6-2T**
Class V1 — MRN 6/64

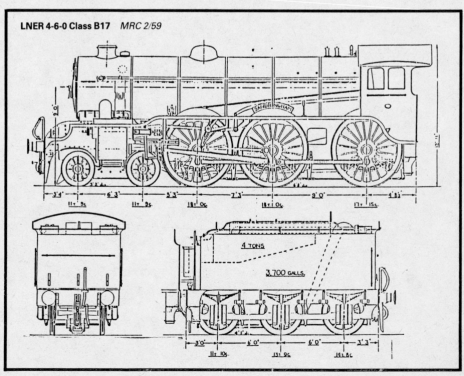

**LNER 4-6-0 Class B17** *MRC 2/59*

**NER 0-4-4T Class O – LNER Class G5**   *MRC 9/60*

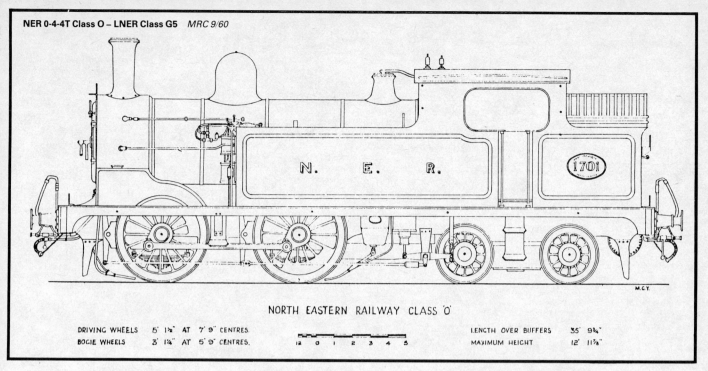

NORTH EASTERN RAILWAY CLASS 'O'

| | | |
|---|---|---|
| DRIVING WHEELS | 5' 1½" AT 7' 9" CENTRES. | LENGTH OVER BUFFERS   35' 9¼" |
| BOGIE WHEELS | 3' 1¼" AT 5' 9" CENTRES. | MAXIMUM HEIGHT   12' 11⅝" |

**2-6-4T**
Class L1                         MRY   4/84
Class L3 (ex-GCR)                RM    4/73
**4-6-2T**
Class A5 (ex-GCR)               RM    4/73
**0-8-4T**
Class S1 (ex-GCR)              MRC   3/73
**4-8-0T**
Class T1 (ex-NER)              MRC   6/70
**2-8-8-2T**
Class U1                         RM    5/83

**Railcars**
Railmotor (ex-GNR)              MRC   7/72
Sentinel Steam Railcar 2-cyl
  100hp                          RM    2/73
                                 MRY   9/79
Sentinel Steam Railcar 6-cyl
  100hp                          MRN   5/67
**Electric Loco** (ex-NER, 1904)   MRY   9/75
**25 ton Craven Bros Steam
  Breakdown Crane** (ex-NER)    MRC   6/76
**Stone Platt Turbo-generator**   MRY   1/73

## Absorbed Railways

*Colne Valley & Halstead Railway*
**0-6-2T**
No 5 (LNER Class N18)           MRC   3/62

*Great Central Railway*
**4-2-2**
Class 13 (LNER Class X4)        MRN   7/67
**4-4-0**
Class 11B (LNER Class D9)       MRN   9/63

**GNR Railcar No 2**   *MRC 7/72*

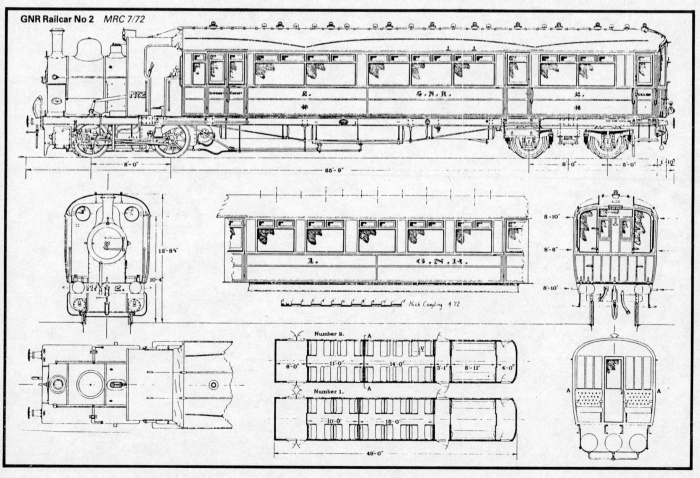

**Class 11E (LNER Class D10)** — RM 9/68
**Class 11F (LNER Class D11)** — MRC 1/62; RM 8/69; MRY 5/74

**4-4-2**
Class 9L (LNER Class C14) — RM 6/67
**0-6-0**
ex-MSLR — MRN 3/65
Class 9J (LNER Class J11) — MRN 6/62; MRC 1/70
**2-6-0**
Baldwin — RM 5/85
**4-6-0**
Class 8 (LNER Class B5) — MRN 1/64
Class 8F (LNER Class B4) — MRC 9/63
Class 9P (LNER Class B3) — RM 10/72
**0-8-0**
Class 8K (LNER Class 04) — MRN 11/61; RM 10/65
**2-8-0**
Class 8A (LNER Class Q4) — MRN 2/63
**0-4-4T**
Class C (LNER Class G3) — MRC 3/76; MRC 8/76
**2-4-2T**
Class 3 (LNER Class F1) — RM 11/67
**4-4-2T**
Class 9K (LNER Class C13) — RM 6/67; RM 11/68
**0-6-0T**
No 401 (ex-WMCQ No 8) — RM 11/66
**0-6-0ST**
ex MSLR (LNER Class J58) — MRC 12/68
Class 18T (LNER Class J59) — MRC 12/68
**0-6-2T**
Class 9A (LNER Class N4) — RM 11/70
Class 9F (LNER Class N5) — RM 11/70
**0-6-4T**
Class D (LNER Class M1) — RM 4/78
**2-6-4T**
Class 1B (LNER Class L3) — RM 4/73
**4-6-2T**
Class 9N (LNER Class A5) — RM 4/73
**0-8-4T**
Class 8H (LNER Class S1) — MRY 3/73

*Great Eastern Railway*
**4-2-2** — MRN 5/63
**2-4-0**
Class T19 — RM 12/64
Class T26 (LNER Class E4) — MRY 2/84
**4-4-0**
'Ironclads' — MRN 10/62
**2-6-0**
No 527 — MRN 3/62
**0-4-0T**
Class G15 (LNER Class Y6) — RM 7/61; MRY 3/84
**0-4-0ST**
Class 209 (LNER Class Y5) — MRY 8/72
**0-4-2T**
Class T7 — MRY 12/82
**2-4-2T**
Class M15 (LNER Class F4) — MRY 3/76
**0-6-0T**
Class R24 (LNER Class J67) — MRY 1/84
Class R24R (LNER Class J69) — MRY 3/72; MRY 11/82

*Great Northern Railway*
**2-2-2**
Hawthorn (1847) — RM 6/73
Hawthorn Tender Express — RM 10/73

Stirling (1868) — RM 5/72
Sharp Stewart (1847) — MRN 10/60
**4-2-2**
*Lovett Eames* (Baldwin) — RM 11/66
Stirling 8′ Single — RM 5/73; RM 12/83
**0-4-2**
No 551 — MRN 10/64
**2-4-0**
Sharp Stewart Passenger (1865) — RM 5/74
Stirling — RM 6/72
**4-4-0**
Class D1 (LNER Class D2) — RM 12/72; MRY 11/84
**4-4-2**
Class C1 — MRC 5/60
Class C1 (LNER Class C2) — RM 2/75
**0-6-0**
Goods (1854) — RM 6/74
Hawthorn (1850) — RM 5/73
Hawthorn Steam Tender — RM 8/73
Sturrock Steam Tender No 2 — RM 12/73
No 1027 (1896) — MRC 9/60
No 142 (1887) — MRC 9/60
No 1092 (1897) — MRC 9/60
Stirling Large Cylinder — RM 11/73
**2-6-0**
Class H3 (LNER Class K2) — MRY 3/75
Baldwin — RM 5/85
**4-6-2**
Class A1 — MRC 8/60; MRY 4/72
**2-8-0**
Class 01 — RM 8/72
Class 02 — RM 8/72
**0-4-2WT**
Neilson (1866) — RM 1/75
**4-4-2T**
Class C2 (LNER Class C12) — MRC 8/71
**0-6-0T**
Class J23 (LNER Class J50) — MRN 2/69
**0-6-0ST**
Class J13 (LNER Class J52) — MRN 4/65
**0-6-2T**
Class N2 — RM 4/77; RM 9/82; MRC 7/72
**Railmotor**
**4-Wheel Bogies**
Stirling — MRY 7/75
Swing Link — MRY 10/75

*Great North of Scotland Railway*
**4-4-0**
Class S (LNER Class D41) — MRN 4/63
Class V (LNER Class D40) — MRN 7/61
**0-4-2T**
Class Y (LNER Class Z5) — MRC 7/68

*Hull & Barnsley Railway*
**0-6-0**
Beyer Peacock (1885) — MRN 1/68
Class L (LNER Class J28) — RM 9/76
**0-8-0**
Class A (LNER Class Q10) — RM 3/79
**0-6-0T**
No 12 — MRN 7/66

*Midland & Great Northern Railway*
**0-6-0**
Class D (LNER Class J40) — MRN 10/63
**4-4-0T**
Class B — MRC 3/71
**4-4-2T**
Class A (LNER Class C17) — MRC 2/60

**0-6-0T**
(LNER Class J93) — MRC 4/71
No 16A — MRC 2/71

*North British Railway*
**0-4-0**
Class G Rebuilt (LNER Class Y10) — RM 10/66
**4-4-0**
Class M (LNER Class D31) — RM 2/66
Class K (LNER Class D34) — RM 12/68
**4-4-2**
Class H (LNER Class C11) — RM 3/76
**0-6-0**
Class B (LNER Class J35) — RM 3/68
Class S (LNER Class J37) — MRN 8/62; RM 5/68; MRY 3/72
**0-4-0ST**
Class G (LNER Class Y9) — MRN 10/67
**4-4-0T**
Class P (LNER Class D50) — MRN 1/62
**0-6-0T**
Class D (LNER Class J83) — MRN 2/65
**0-6-2T**
Class A (LNER Class N15) — MRN 2/64; RM 9/67

*North Eastern Railway*
**2-4-0**
Class 901 (LNER Class E6) — RM 9/75; MRY 1/77
**4-4-0**
Lowther (ex-S&DR) — MRN 7/60
No 1160 *Brougham* — MRN 12/60
'Whitby Bogie' – Rebuilt — MRN 6/60
Class M – 3CC (LNER Class D19) — MRC 3/60
**0-6-0**
Sharp Stewart (1860) — RM 5/75
No 1681 (Tender Cab-Rebuilt) — MRY 9/83
No 1743 (RSH Rebuilt) — MRY 9/83
No 1112 (ex-S&DR *Lion*) — MRY 9/83
No 1253 — MRY 9/83
No 1229 (ex-S&DR) — MRY 10/83
No 1094 (ex-S&DR) — MRY 10/83
Class 93 — MRY 8/78
Class 1001 — MRY 9/75; MRY 10/83
Class P3 (LNER Class J27) — RM 6/66
**4-6-2**
Class 4-6-2 (LNER Class A2) — RM 1/85
**0-8-0**
Class T (LNER Class Q5) — MRN 12/65
**0-4-0T**
Class H (LNER Class Y7) — RM 7/72
Class K (LNER Class Y8) — MRC 11/59; MRN 1/69; RM 7/72
**0-4-4T**
Class O (LNER Class G5) — MRC 9/60
Class BTP (LNER Class G6) — MRY 7/79
**2-4-2T**
Class A (LNER Class F8) — RM 9/72
**0-6-0T**
Class 964 — RM 7/70
Nos 518 & 519 — MRY 9/78
**0-6-2T**
Class B1 (LNER Class N8) — RM 7/71
Class N (LNER Class N9) — RM 7/71
Class U (LNER Class N10) — RM 7/71
**4-8-0T**
Class X (LNER Class T1) — MRC 6/70
**Electric Loco (1904)** — MRY 9/75
**4 Wheel Bogie** — MRY 11/75

# Coaching Stock

### London & North Eastern Railway

**61'6″ Corridor Stock – Gresley:**

| | | |
|---|---|---|
| Open Third (Diag 186) | RM | 10/66 |
| Brake Third (Diags 37A, 40A, 114, 178) | MRC | 11/66 |
| Brake Composite (Diags 31, 134, 175) | MRY | 9/71 |
| Restaurant-Buffet Car (Diag 275) | MRN | 4/66 |
| Buffet Car (Diag 167) | MRC | 4/67 |
| Composite Sleeping Car (Diag 74A) | MRC | 2/73 |
| Brake Van (Diag 260) | RM | 6/67 |

**63' Corridor Stock – Thompson:**

| | | |
|---|---|---|
| Composite | MRC | 4/64 |
| Brake Composite | MRC | 4/64 |
| Brake Third | MRC | 4/64 |
| Full Brake | MRC | 4/64 |

**Non-Corridor Stock – Thompson:**

| | | |
|---|---|---|
| Composite | MRC | 2/66 |
| Third | MRC | 2/66 |
| Brake Third | MRC | 8/66 |
| Quad-Art Set | MRC | 5/66 |
| 4 wheel Covered Carriage Truck (Diag 6) | MRY | 5/83 |

### East Coast Joint Stock

**Corridor Stock – Clerestory Roof:**

| | | |
|---|---|---|
| Composite (Diag 2) | MRC | 9/69 |
| Composite (Diag 6) | MRC | 6/65 |
| 12 wheel Third (Diag 27) | MRC | 6/65 |
| Third (Diag 14) | MRC | 5/69 |
| 12 wheel Open Third (Diag 28) | MRC | 11/65 |
| 12 wheel Brake Third (Diag 51) | MRC | 12/64 |
| 12 wheel Brake Third (Diag 54) | MRY | 10/74 |
| 12 wheel First Dining Saloon (Diag 76A) | MRC | 11/65 |
| 12 wheel First Dining Saloon (Diag 77) | MRC | 11/65 |
| 12 wheel Third Dining Saloon (Diag 30) | MRC | 11/65 |
| 12 wheel First Sleeping Car (Diag 62) | MRC | 3/68 |
| First Sleeping Car (Diag 66) | MRC | 4/68 |
| First Sleeping Car (Diag 67) | MRC | 8/68 |
| Composite Sleeping Car (Diag 72) | MRC | 2/69 |
| 12 wheel Composite Sleeping Car (Diag 73) | MRC | 3/68 |

### Great Central Railway

| | | |
|---|---|---|
| Corridor First (1889) | RM | 1/81 |
| Van Composite (1899) | RM | 8/82 |
| Brake Third (1899) | RM | 8/82 |
| Buffet Car | RM | 6/81 |
| 50' Composite – Clerestory | MRC | 4/69 |
| 50' Brake Third – Clerestory | MRC | 4/69 |
| 56' First | MRC | 7/60 |
| 60' Third | MRC | 7/60 |
| 60' Brake Composite | MRC | 7/60 |
| 60' Push-Pull Trailer (ex-Steam Rail Motor) | RM | 11/68 |
| 53' Push-Pull Trailer Composite | RM | 11/68 |

**6 wheel ex-LDECR Stock (1896-1898):**

| | | |
|---|---|---|
| Composite Saloon | MRC | 3/76 |
| | MRC | 8/76 |
| Luggage Composite | MRC | 3/76 |
| | MRC | 8/76 |
| Third | MRC | 3/76 |
| | MRC | 8/76 |
| Brake Third | MRC | 3/76 |
| | MRC | 8/76 |

### Great Eastern Railway

| | | |
|---|---|---|
| 4 wheel Third (1882) | MRY | 10/74 |
| 6 wheel Parliamentary (ex-Eastern Counties R) | MRC | 7/70 |
| 6 wheel Parliamentary (ex-Yarmouth & Norwich R) | MRC | 1/69 |

**50' Corridor Stock:**

| | | |
|---|---|---|
| Composite | MRC | 4/63 |
| Third | MRC | 4/63 |
| Brake Third | MRC | 4/63 |
| 4 wheel Covered Carriage Truck | RM | 6/70 |

### Great Northern Railway

| | | |
|---|---|---|
| 6 wheel Third | MRY | 6/78 |
| 6 wheel Brake Third | MRC | 3/84 |

**Corridor Stock – Clerestory Roof:**

| | | |
|---|---|---|
| 52' Open Third (Diag 24) | MRY | 6/82 |
| 51' Open Third | MRC | 2/64 |
| Semi-Open First | MRC | 7/81 |
| 12 wheel Composite | MRC | 8/81 |
| 12 wheel Brake First | MRC | 12/79 |
| 63' 12 wheel Brake Composite Semi-Open | MRC | 9/81 |
| 64' 12 wheel Brake Composite Semi-Open | MRC | 3/82 |
| 12' wheel Brake Third Open (Diag 285D) | MRC | 11/79 |
| 12' wheel Brake Third Open | MRC | 10/81 |
| Luggage Brake Van | MRC | 1/77 |
| Post Office Van | MRC | 9/76 |

**Corridor Stock – Elliptical Roof:**

| | | |
|---|---|---|
| Composite (Diag 109) | MRC | 7/77 |
| 12 wheel Composite | MRC | 12/78 |
| Open Third – Sheffield Stock (Diag 224) | MRC | 7/77 |
| Brake First – Sheffield Stock (Diag 96) | MRC | 6/77 |
| Brake Third – Sheffield Stock (Diag 256) | MRC | 6/77 |
| Brake Composite (Diag 175) | MRC | 12/78 |
| Brake Third/Corr Composite, articulated | MRC | 9/82 |
| Brake Pantry Third/Composite – articulated | MRC | 9/82 |
| Sleeping Car – GN/NE Joint (Diag 17) | MRC | 2/73 |
| Luggage Brake Van | MRC | 7/66 |
| | MRC | 11/76 |
| Post Office Van | MRC | 9/76 |

**Non-Corridor Stock – Elliptical Roof:**

| | | |
|---|---|---|
| Composite (Diag 121) | MRY | 10/75 |
| Saloon Third (Diag 21) | MRY | 10/75 |
| Brake Composite (Diag 183) | MRY | 10/75 |
| Brake Van (Diag 307) | MRY | 10/75 |
| Luggage/Milk Brake (Diag 310) | MRY | 10/75 |
| Brake Third (Diag 274) | MRY | 10/75 |

**Articulated Suburban Stock:**

| | | |
|---|---|---|
| Twin Composite | MRC | 8/82 |
| Twin Third | MRC | 8/82 |
| Brake Third/Third | MRC | 7/82 |
| 6 wheel Full Brake | MRC | 7/84 |
| Horse Box | RM | 5/59 |

### Great North of Scotland Railway

| | | |
|---|---|---|
| 54' Corridor Brake Composite | MRC | 1/63 |

### Hull & Barnsley Railway

| | | |
|---|---|---|
| Composite | MRC | 1/61 |
| Third | MRC | 1/61 |
| Brake Composite | MRC | 1/61 |
| Brake Composite | MRC | 2/65 |
| Brake Third | MRC | 2/65 |

### Midland & Great Northern Joint Railway

**6 wheel Stock:**

| | | |
|---|---|---|
| Brake Third (ex-GNR) | MRC | 3/84 |
| Full Brake (ex-GNR) | MRC | 7/84 |
| Full Brake (M&GN built) | MRC | 5/84 |

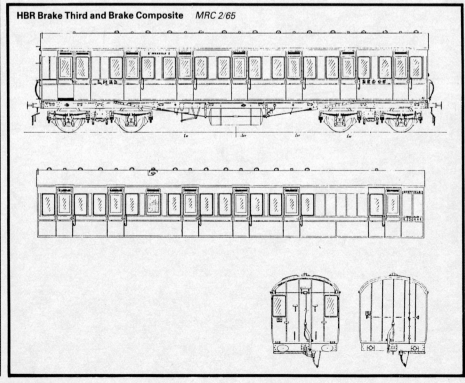

HBR Brake Third and Brake Composite *MRC 2/65*

## Freight Stock

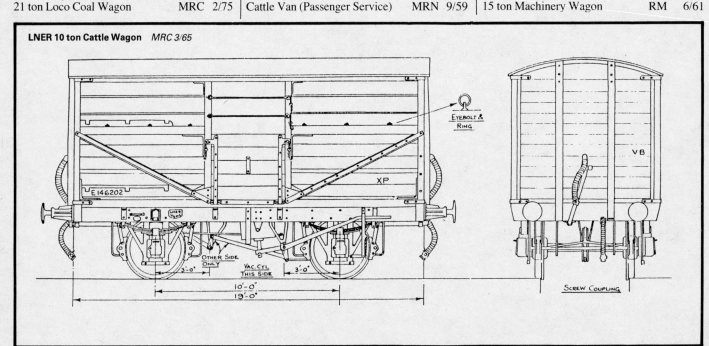

**LNER 10 ton Cattle Wagon** *MRC 3/65*

E 146202 — XP — EYEBOLT & RING — OTHER SIDE ONLY — VAC. CYL. THIS SIDE — 3'-0" — 10'-0" — 19'-0" — VB — SCREW COUPLING

| | | |
|---|---|---|
| 20 ton Loco Coal Wagon | MRC | 3/76 |
| 50 ton Bogie Brick Wagon | MRC | 3/75 |
| Single Bolster Wagon | RM | 6/61 |
| Double Bolster Wagon | RM | 6/61 |
| Portable Engine Wagon | RM | 6/61 |
| Shunters Truck | MRC | 2/63 |

*Great North of Scotland Railway*

| | | |
|---|---|---|
| 12 ton Van | MRC | 6/64 |
| 8 ton Bolster (timber) Wagon | MRN | 6/66 |
| 10 ton 3 plank Open Wagon | MRN | 11/64 |
| 10 ton high-sided Open Wagon | MRC | 9/72 |

*Hull & Barnsley Railway*

| | | |
|---|---|---|
| Ventilated Van | RM | 4/60 |
| | MRC | 7/65 |
| 10 ton Brake Van | RM | 4/60 |
| 10 ton Open Wagon | MRC | 10/68 |
| 10 ton high-sided Open Wagon | MRN | 3/63 |
| 10 ton Double Bolster (timber) Wagon | MRN | 12/62 |

*Midland & Great Northern Joint Railway*

| | | |
|---|---|---|
| 8 ton low-sided Goods Wagon | RM | 12/74 |
| Ballast Wagon (ex-Lynn & Fakenham Railway) | MRN | 7/69 |

*North British Railway*

| | | |
|---|---|---|
| 6 ton Van | MRC | 9/65 |
| 8 ton Vans | MRN | 8/63 |
| | MRN | 11/63 |
| | MRN | 12/63 |
| | MRN | 7/64 |
| 10 ton Van | RM | 3/73 |
| Cattle Van | RM | 9/59 |
| | MRC | 9/65 |
| 6 wheel Van | MRC | 1/65 |
| 6 wheel Brake Van | MRC | 3/66 |
| 8 ton low-sided Open Wagon | MRN | 8/60 |
| 8 ton medium drop-side Wagon | MRN | 5/67 |
| 8 ton end-door Coal Wagon | MRN | 10/62 |
| 10 ton end-door Coal Wagon | MRC | 12/70 |
| | RM | 9/73 |
| 10 ton Bar Iron Wagon | MRN | 12/59 |
| 16 ton Mineral Wagon | MRC | 1/76 |
| 16 ton end-door Coal Wagon | RM | 1/74 |
| 40 ton Trolley Wagon | MRN | 9/59 |
| Livestock Wagon | MRN | 4/67 |
| Ballast Wagon | RM | 9/59 |

*North Eastern Railway*

| | | |
|---|---|---|
| 8 ton Van | MRN | 4/65 |
| 8 ton Refrigerator Van | MRC | 8/64 |
| 10 ton Ventilated Van | MRC | 6/69 |
| 10 ton medium Cattle Van | MRN | 6/62 |
| 12 ton Van | MRN | 9/60 |
| 10 ton Brake Van | MRC | 1/66 |
| Brake Vans (Birdcage) | MRY | 9/75 |
| Ballast Brake Van | MRC | 5/65 |
| 10½ ton Mineral Van | MRC | 5/67 |
| 10½ ton Hopper Wagon | RM | 6/59 |
| 12 ton high-sided Goods Wagon | RM | 9/75 |
| 12 ton Hopper Wagon | RM | 6/59 |
| 12 ton Plate Wagon | MRY | 6/72 |
| 20 ton Hopper Wagon | RM | 6/59 |
| 20 ton Bogie Trolley Wagon | MRN | 4/66 |
| 20 ton Bogie Pulley Wagon | RM | 6/81 |
| 25 ton Bogie Plate Wagon | MRY | 6/72 |
| 40 ton Bogie Mineral Wagons | MRY | 12/77 |
| 40 ton Bogie Trolley Wagon | MRC | 10/68 |
| Drop-side Wagon | RM | 6/59 |
| Stone Ballast Wagon | MRC | 7/65 |
| Twin Bolster Wagon | RM | 2/75 |
| Agricultural Implement Wagon | RM | 11/82 |
| Gas Tank Wagon | RM | 3/83 |

**GNR Brick Built Signal Cabin** *MRC 1/75*

# Structures

*London & North Eastern Railway*

| | | |
|---|---|---|
| Coaling Tower (Concrete) | RM | 5/67 |
| Platelayer's Hut (Concrete) | MRY | 3/75 |
| Telegraph Poles | MRY | 4/75 |
| Signalbox Nameboard | MRC | 10/74 |
| Battery Boxes | MRC | 2/75 |
| Signals | MRN | 3/63 |
| | MRC | 1/65 |
| | MRY | 4/72 |
| | MRC | 1/85 |
| Signals Summary | MRC | 6/84 |

*Cheshire Lines Committee*

| | | |
|---|---|---|
| Signalbox – Delamere | MRC | 5/74 |
| Station Nameboard | RM | 1/73 |
| Signals | MRN | 5/63 |
| | MRN | 2/69 |
| | MRC | 1/85 |
| Signals Summary | MRC | 6/84 |

*Great Central Railway*

| | | |
|---|---|---|
| Island Platform Stations (Lutterworth – Quorn) | MRC | 2/75 |
| Station Nameboard | MRN | 2/69 |
| | RM | 7/66 |
| Signalbox – Deepcar | RM | 6/61 |
| Goods Shed | MRC | 7/76 |
| Footbridge | MRC | 2/72 |
| Buffer Stops | MRC | 9/65 |
| Weighbridge | MRC | 7/76 |
| Signals | MRN | 5/63 |
| | MRC | 1/85 |
| Signals Summary | MRC | 6/84 |

*Great Eastern Railway*

| | | |
|---|---|---|
| Station Nameboard | RM | 7/66 |
| Station Valance | MRN | 2/62 |

| | | |
|---|---|---|
| Signalbox – Wood | MRC | 11/74 |
| Platform Signalbox – Brick | MRC | 12/74 |
| Platform Signalbox – Wood | MRC | 12/74 |
| Signalbox – Brick | MRC | 11/74 |
| Signalbox – Hadham | RM | 11/78 |
| Signal Hut – Block Station | MRC | 2/75 |
| Crossing Keeper's House | MRY | 9/72 |
| Porter's Hut | RM | 4/71 |
| Goods Yard Office – Buntingford | RM | 8/73 |
| Platform Seats | MRC | 10/66 |
| Level Crossing Gates | MRY | 7/72 |
| Water Tower | MRC | 4/72 |
| Wagon Turntable | MRY | 4/73 |
| Signal Finial | MRN | 8/62 |
| Signals | MRN | 5/63 |
| | MRN | 8/63 |
| | MRC | 1/85 |
| Signals Summary | MRC | 6/84 |

*Great Northern Railway*

**Stations:**

| | | |
|---|---|---|
| Horncastle | MRC | 3/61 |
| Peterborough | MRY | 5/74 |
| Stamford | RM | 2/76 |
| Station Nameboard | RM | 7/66 |

**Signal Boxes:**

| | | |
|---|---|---|
| Typical | MRC | 3/72 |
| Wood-built | MRC | 1/75 |
| Brick-built | MRC | 1/75 |
| Biggleswade | MRC | 8/75 |
| High Dyke | RM | 6/78 |
| Three Counties | MRC | 9/74 |
| Weighbridge Office | MRC | 7/74 |
| Coal Office | MRC | 7/74 |
| Buffer Stop | RM | 7/83 |
| Mile Post | RM | 7/83 |
| Gradient Post | RM | 7/83 |
| Fencing | MRC | 4/75 |

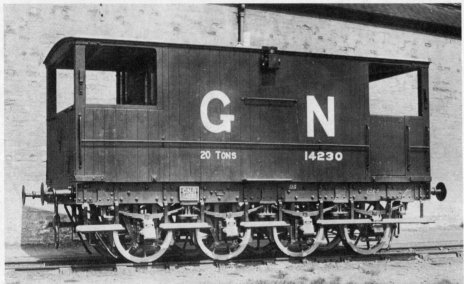

*Above:* **LNER Gresley 'A4' class 4-6-2 No 4462 William Whitelaw**. (Drawings RM 9/71, MRY 7/76, MRC 3/75, 5/75 and 8/75).
*Real Photographs (1493)*

*Left:* **Great Northern Railway 20 ton 8 wheel brake van No 14230**. (Drawing MRC 7/66).
*LNER/Ian Allan Library*

*Below left:* **North British Railway Class G 0-4-0ST as British Railways 'Y9' class No 68115 with wooden tender**. (Drawing MRN 10/67).
*W. S. Sellar*

# Southern Railway

## Locomotives

**4-4-0**
| | | |
|---|---|---|
| Class L1 | MRN | 1/61 |

**0-6-0**
| | | |
|---|---|---|
| Class O | MRY | 10/74 |

**4-6-0**
| | | |
|---|---|---|
| Class N15 'King Arthur' | RM | 1/61 |
| | MRY | 1/78 |
| | MRY | 2/78 |

**4-6-2**
| | | |
|---|---|---|
| 'Merchant Navy' Class – rebuilt | MRY | 7/72 |
| 'West Country' Class – unrebuilt | MRY | 8/74 |
| | MRY | 9/74 |
| 'West Country' Class – rebuilt | MRN | 9/60 |

**2-6-4T**
| | | |
|---|---|---|
| Class W | MRC | 1/64 |
| | RM | 11/84 |

**0-8-0T**
| | | |
|---|---|---|
| Class Z | RM | 9/80 |
| **350hp Diesel-electric** (English Electric) | MRY | 4/76 |
| **Drewry Petrol Railcar No 5** | MRC | 5/76 |
| **5 ton Taylor Hubbard Crane** (Meldon Quarry) | MRC | 8/80 |

## Absorbed Railways

*London, Brighton & South Coast Railway*

**2-2-2**
| | | |
|---|---|---|
| No 14 | MRN | 3/60 |

**2-4-0**
| | | |
|---|---|---|
| Hove | MRN | 9/61 |

**0-6-0**
| | | |
|---|---|---|
| DeWinton Class altered, Manning Wardle (1866) | MRY | 8/77 |
| Class A | RM | 12/81 |
| Class D2 | MRY | 2/73 |

**2-6-0**
| | | |
|---|---|---|
| Class K | MRY | 9/77 |
| | RM | 7/84 |

**2-2-2T**
| | | |
|---|---|---|
| No 97 | MRN | 10/69 |

**0-4-4T**
| | | |
|---|---|---|
| Class D3 | MRN | 4/64 |

**4-6-2T**
| | | |
|---|---|---|
| Class J1 | RM | 12/82 |

*London & South Western Railway*

**4-2-2-0**
| | | |
|---|---|---|
| Class E10 | RM | 1/70 |

| | | |
|---|---|---|
| Class T7 | RM | 1/70 |

**0-4-2**
| | | |
|---|---|---|
| 'Jubilee' Class | MRN | 5/67 |
| | RM | 9/75 |

**2-4-0**
| | | |
|---|---|---|
| Sharp (1867) | MRN | 9/67 |

**4-4-0**
| | | |
|---|---|---|
| Class C8 | RM | 1/73 |
| Class K10 | RM | 10/70 |
| Class L11 | RM | 10/70 |
| Class L12 | RM | 7/84 |
| Class T3 Adams | MRN | 3/66 |
| Class T9 | MRN | 2/64 |
| | MRC | 2/68 |
| Class T9 Tender | MRN | 8/64 |
| Class 0460 Adams | MRN | 10/61 |

**0-6-0**
| | | |
|---|---|---|
| 'Ilfracombe Goods' | MRN | 9/69 |
| Class 700 | MRN | 6/63 |

**4-6-0**
| | | |
|---|---|---|
| Class T14 | RM | 7/72 |
| Class T14 – rebuilt | RM | 7/72 |
| Class N15 'King Arthur' | RM | 1/61 |
| | MRY | 1/78 |
| | MRY | 2/78 |

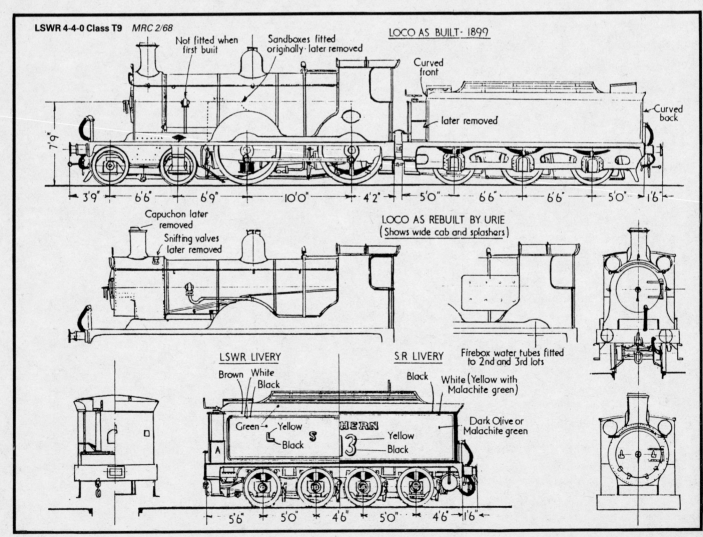

**LSWR 4-4-0 Class T9** *MRC 2/68*

LOCO AS BUILT · 1899

Not fitted when first built

Sandboxes fitted originally · later removed

Curved front

later removed

Curved back

7'9"

3'9" — 6'6" — 6'9" — 10'0" — 4'2" — 5'0" — 6'6" — 6'6" — 5'0" — 1'6"

Capuchon later removed

Snifting valves later removed

LOCO AS REBUILT BY URIE (Shows wide cab and splashers)

Firebox water tubes fitted to 2nd and 3rd lots

LSWR LIVERY

Brown White Black

Green Yellow Black

S.R. LIVERY

Black

White (Yellow with Malachite green)

Dark Olive or Malachite green

Yellow Black

5'6" — 5'0" — 4'6" — 5'0" — 4'6" — 1'6"

**2-2-0T**
Class C14 — RM 8/68

**0-4-0T**
Class C14 – rebuilt — RM 8/68
Class B4 — MRY 12/71

**0-4-0ST**
No 1 *Bodmin* (Bodmin & Wadebridge Railway) — MRY 9/76

**2-4-0WT**
*Phoenix* (1872) — MRY 5/82
No 248 — MRY 5/82
Class 0298 — MRC 5/67 / MRC 2/70

**0-4-4T**
Class O2 — MRN 3/60 / RM 8/68
Class M7 — RM 8/68 / RM 6/82 / MRY 10/84
Class M7 (Rebuilt) No 126 — RM 8/68

**4-4-2T**
Class 0415 — MRY 9/77
Adams Radial — MRY 9/82 / RM 8/83

**0-6-0T**
Class G6 — RM 6/67

**0-6-0ST**
Class 0330 — MRC 2/72

**4-6-2T**
Class H16 — RM 12/69

**4-2-4T**
Class F9 – Inspection Saloon — MRC 8/68
**Class H13 Railmotor** — MRC 10/78
**Electric No 748** — MRC 3/59

*South Eastern & Chatham Railway*
**2-4-0**
Class C (Sharp Stewart) — MRY 10/71

**4-4-0**
Class D — MRY 3/84
Class E1 — MRC 11/61
Class L1 — MRN 1/61
Nos 676-680 — MRN 7/61
Ex-LCDR No 157 — MRN 2/62

**0-6-0**
Class B2 (ex-LCDR) — MRN 12/62
Class C — MRN 12/68
Class O — MRN 8/71
Class O1 — MRN 8/71

**0-4-0ST**
No 313 — MRY 9/72

**0-4-4T**
Class H — MRY 8/76
Class Q — MRN 7/71
Class Q1 — MRN 7/71
Class R1 — MRN 9/62

**0-6-0T**
Class T (ex-LCDR) — MRN 5/64
**Railmotor Nos 1-8** — MRC 3/64
**Railmotor** (Sheppy Line) — RM 9/75
**4 Wheel Bogie** (Stirling) — MRY 8/75

# Coaching Stock

*Southern Railway*
**Bulleid Stock:**
Corridor First — MRC 6/67 / RM 9/75
Corridor Composite — MRC 3/67 / MRC 1/81
Corridor Composite (BRCW) — MRC 12/80
Corridor Third — MRC 4/67 / MRC 1/81
Corridor Third (BRCW) — MRC 12/80


Open Saloon Third — MRC 8/67
Brake Composite — MRC 2/67
Brake Composite – Loose — MRC 9/67
Brake Third — MRC 1/67 / MRC 1/81
Semi-Open Brake Third — MRC 1/67
Semi-Open Brake Third (BRCW) — MRC 12/80
Dining First — MRC 10/67
Kitchen-Dining Third — MRC 11/67
Tavern Car Set — MRC 1/71
Tavern Car Set (Rebuilt) — MRC 11/80
Underframe — MRC 5/67
Bogie — MRC 5/67

**Maunsell Corridor Stock:**
First — MRC 3/66
Composite — MRC 3/65
Third — MRC 3/65
Brake Third — MRC 3/65
Pantry Brake First — MRC 3/66
Luggage Van — MRC 9/65
Unclassified Saloons (ex-LSWR Dining Saloons) — MRC 1/75 / MRC 5/75

**Push-Pull Stock converted from LBSCR Electric Stock:**
Third — MRC 1/80
Trailer Third — MRC 4/82
Driving Trailer Composite — MRC 4/82
Push-Pull Set (BR) — MRC 11/72
Pullman Car *Hibernia* – Cravens (1914) — MRC 5/77

**Isle of Wight Stock – ex LBSCR:**
Composite — MRC 7/63
Third — MRC 6/66
Brake Thirds — MRC 7/63
4 wheel Utility Van PMV (SECR type) — RM 11/73
4 wheel Utility Van PMV (1400 type) — RM 11/73
4 wheel Utility Van Type B7 — RM 6/74
4 wheel Brake Van — RM 4/74
4 wheel Birdcage Brake Van — RM 6/74
6 wheel 32' Covered Carriage Truck — RM 10/80
Corridor PMV — RM 1/74
Brake Utility Van Type B — MRC 12/66 / RM 6/74


General Utility Van Type BY — MRY 4/72
Brake Van — RM 4/74
IoW Luggage Brake (Conv SECR Brake Third) — RM 6/74
'Night Ferry' Baggage Vans – SNCF — RM 11/75
Naval Ambulance Saloon (Conv Unclass Saloon) — MRC 1/75 / MRC 5/75

**Electric Multiple Units:**
4-COR:
Motor Brake Second — MRC 3/65 / MCR 7/73
Trailer Composite — MRC 5/65 / MRC 7/73
Trailer Second — MRC 5/65 / MRC 7/73
2-BIL — MRC 4/70
2-NOL — MRC 10/68
**South London Stock:**
Driving Trailer Composite — MRN 10/66
Motor Coach Third — MRN 10/66
AC Power Van — MRN 7/64

*Isle of Wight Central Railway*
Composite (1889) — MRY 6/72
Brake Third (1889) — MRY 6/72

*London, Brighton & South Coast Railway*
4 wheel Parliamentary (ex-BCDR) — MRC 11/68
4 wheel Suburban Set — MRC 4/72
**4 wheel Block Set (1872):**
26' First — MRC 4/77
26' Second — MRC 4/77
26' Third — MRC 4/77
26' Brake Third — MRC 4/77
6 wheel First — MRN 10/64
6 wheel Saloon First — MRC 1/72
6 wheel Second — MRN 12/64
6 wheel Composite (First/Second) — MRN 12/64
6 wheel Third — MRN 10/64 / MRC 5/72
6 wheel Brake Third — MRN 1/65
6 wheel Brake Second Slip — MRN 1/65
**48' Stock:**
Composite — MRC 8/72
Third – 8 Compartment — MRC 8/72

**SR 2-NOL Electric Unit**  *MRC 10/68*

Motor brake third

Driving trailer composite

**Third – 9 Compartment** — MRC 1/80
**Brake Third** — MRC 8/72

**54′ Stock:**
Tricomposite — MRC 11/71
Composite (First/Second) — MRC 12/71
Second — MRC 12/71
Third — MRC 11/71
Brake First — MRC 11/71
Brake Third — MRC 11/71
— MRC 7/72

**'Baloon Stock':**
Composite — MRC 1/73
Brake Third — MRC 1/73

**Brighton Stock:**
Composite — MRC 8/76
Brake Third — MRC 8/76

**Push-Pull Units:**
Trailer Composite (1909) — MRC 1/80
Trailer Composite (1911) — MRC 2/80
Trailer Composite (1914) — MRC 9/80
Trailer Composite (1921) — MRC 10/80
Trailer Composite (1922) — MRC 2/82
Trailer Brake Third (1911) — MRC 2/80
Trailer Brake Third (1912) — MRC 9/80
Trailer Brake Third (1921) — MRC 10/80
Trailer Brake Third (1922) — MRC 2/82
Composite – 8 Compartment — MRC 7/63
Brake Second — MRC 7/63
Royal Train Set — MRC 6/75
4 wheel Brake Van – Stroudley — MRN 11/64
6 wheel Brake Van – Stroudley — MRN 7/64
6 wheel Brake Van (Stroudley) – Rebuilt Billington — MRN 7/64
6 wheel Brake Van (Billington) — MRN 9/64
6 wheel Double Ended Brake Van (Billington) — MRN 9/64

**Pullman Cars:**
*Albert Edward* — MRC 2/81
*Albert Victor* — MRC 3/72 / MRC 3/81
*Alexandra* — MRC 2/81
*Arundel* — MRC 6/81
*Beatrice* — MRC 2/81
*Chichester* — MRC 6/81
*Devonshire* — MRC 6/81
*Duchess of York* — MRC 5/81

*Empress* — MRC 4/81
*Globe* — MRC 2/81
*Her Majesty* — MRC 5/81
*Jupiter* — MRC 2/81
*Louise* — MRC 2/81
*Maud* — MRC 2/81
*Pavillion* — MRC 4/81
*Prince* — MRC 3/81
*Prince Regent* — MRC 4/81
*Princess* — MRC 3/81
*Princess Mary* — MRC 4/81
*Princess of Wales* — MRC 5/81
*Pup – No 80* — MRC 3/81
*Pup – Large Version* — MRC 2/72
*The Queen* — MRC 4/81
*Victoria* — MRC 2/81

*London & South Western Railway*
4 wheel 24′ 6″ Composite (1877) — MRC 2/76
4 wheel 25′ Composite (1876) — MRC 11/75
4 wheel 25′ Brake Third (1876) — MRC 11/75
4 wheel 28′ 6″ Second (1876) — MRC 2/76
6 wheel 29′ 6″ First (1883) — MRC 2/85
6 wheel 30′ Second (1879) — MRC 7/83
6 wheel 30′ Second (1881) — MRC 7/83
6 wheel 30′ Third (1883) — MRC 7/83
6 wheel 32′ First (1882) — MRC 7/83
6 wheel 34′ Third (1882) — MRC 10/83
6 wheel 34′ Brake Third (1882) — MRC 10/83

**6 wheel Block Train:**
First — MRC 6/69
Composite (Second/Third) — MRC 6/69
Third — MRC 6/69
Brake Third — MRC 6/69
42′ Third — MRC 3/71
42′ Brake Third — MRC 3/71
42′ 6″ Tricomposite — MRC 9/84
43′ First — MRC 12/70
45′ Tricomposite — MRC 4/71
45′ Brake Tricomposite — MRC 4/71
46′ First — MRC 10/70
46′ Composite (First/Second) — MRC 2/71
46′6″ Invalid Saloon — MRC 10/71
47′6″ Saloons — MRC 6/73

**48′ Stock:**
Composite — MRC 3/73

Tricomposite (Diag 712) — MRC 11/73
Tricomposite (Diag 1051) — MRC 12/73
Tricomposite — MRC 9/70
Third — MRC 8/70
Third — MRC 3/73
Brake Tricomposite — MRC 12/73
Brake Third — MRC 9/70

**49′ Stock:**
Composite — MRC 11/76
Third — MRC 12/76

**51′ Stock:**
Composite — MRC 11/76
Third – 8 Compartment — MRC 12/76
Third – 9 Compartment — MRC 12/76

**52′ Corridor Stock:**
First — MRC 9/78
Tricomposite — MRC 9/78

**54′ Corridor Stock:**
Composite — MRC 1/74
Tricomposite — MRC 1/74

**56′ Corridor Stock:**
Tricomposite — MRC 4/74
Third — MRC 1/74
Double Brake Tricomposite — MRC 6/74
Brake Third — MRC 1/74 / MRC 4/74
Brake Third (1908) — MRC 12/82
56′ Non-Corridor 4 Car Set — MRC 10/74
56′ Non-Corridor Brake Third — MRC 9/75

**57′ 'Ironclad' Stock:**
First — MRC 7/79
Pantry Third — MRC 8/79
Third — MRC 7/79
Brake Third — MRC 8/79
'Eagle' Saloons — MRC 11/82
'Eagle' Saloon Conversions — MRC 11/82
Cooking Car and Van (Conv 'Eagle' Saloon) — MRC 12/82
Dining Saloons — MRC 1/75 / MRC 4/75
Sleeping Saloon — MRC 9/68

**Electric Multiple-Unit (Converted Steam Stock):**
Composite — MRY 2/85
Motor Composite — MRY 2/85
Motor Third — MRY 2/85

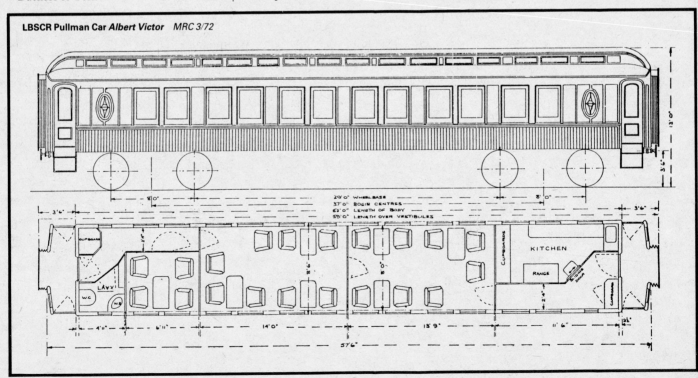

**LBSCR Pullman Car *Albert Victor*** *MRC 3/72*

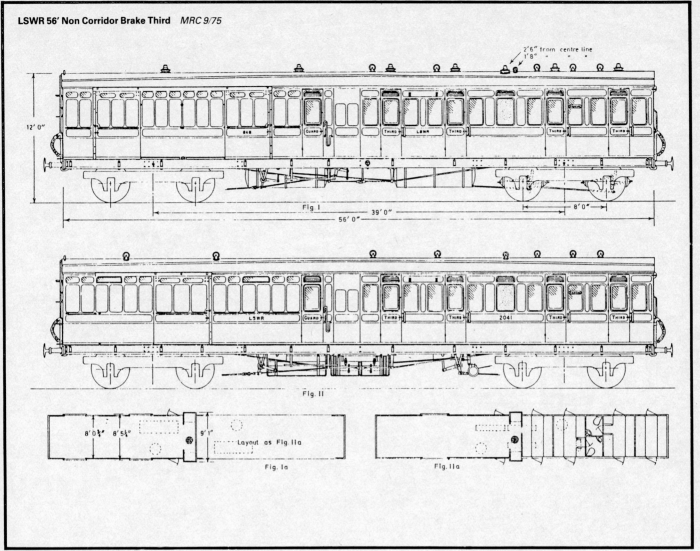

**LSWR 56' Non Corridor Brake Third** *MRC 9/75*

Fig. I

Fig. II

Fig. Ia — Layout as Fig. IIa

Fig. IIa

| | | | | |
|---|---|---|---|---|
| 4 wheel 22' Luggage Van (1883) | MRC 4/76 | **Freight Stock** | | |
| 4 wheel 24' Luggage Van (1887) | MRY 3/75 | | | |
| | MRC 4/76 | *Southern Railway* | | |
| 4 wheel 24' Luggage Van (1894) | MRC 4/76 | 10 ton Refrigerated Van | MRC 4/66 | |
| 4 wheel 24' Special Luggage | | 10 ton Meat Van | MRC 10/66 | |
| Van (1909) | MRC 6/76 | 10 ton Insulated Meat Van | MRC 9/66 | |
| 4 wheel 24' Fruit Van (1896) | MRC 4/76 | 10 ton Banana Van | MRC 8/66 | |
| 4 wheel 24' Hearse Carriage | MRC 10/79 | 12 ton Vans | MRC 12/65 | |
| 16' Horse Box | MRY 7/74 | 12 ton Van (fitted) | MRC 12/65 | |
| 21' Horse Box | MRY 10/74 | Standard Box Van | RM 12/70 | |
| 6 wheel 30' Brake Van | | 25 ton Brake Van | MRC 5/67 | |
| (1882-1885) | MRC 2/83 | | RM 1/71 | |
| 6 wheel 30' Brake Vans | MRC 11/73 | 6 wheel Brake Van (Seaton | | |
| 6 wheel 32' Special Milk Van | MRC 10/79 | Branch) | RM 2/60 | |
| 44' Guards Van | MRC 11/81 | Bogie Brake Van | MRC 9/65 | |
| 44' Bullion Van | MRC 6/84 | | MRC 12/66 | |
| 48' Fruit Van | MRC 11/78 | | RM 3/71 | |
| WD Ambulance Van (Conv from | | 12 ton Standard Open Wagon | MRC 6/64 | |
| 48' Fruit Van) | MRC 11/78 | 12 ton high-sided Wagons | MRC 2/72 | |
| 56' Brake Van (Conv from | | | MRC 4/72 | |
| Ambulance Van) | MRC 10/82 | | MRC 6/72 | |
| | | 20 ton low-sided Wagon | | |
| **Electric Multiple Units:** | | 'Grampus' | MRC 8/61 | |
| Motor Brake Composite | MRC 10/76 | Engineers Ballast Wagon | MRC 12/64 | |
| Motor Brake Third | MRC 10/76 | Tunnel Inspection Truck | MRC 11/64 | |
| | | Stone Block Wagons | MRC 7/65 | |
| *South Eastern & Chatham Railway* | | | | |
| 4 wheel 27' Composite | MRY 4/73 | *London, Brighton & South Coast Railway* | | |
| 4 wheel 27' Third | MRY 4/73 | 8 ton Van | MRN 5/69 | |
| 4 wheel 27' Brake Third | MRY 5/73 | 8 ton Ventilated Van | MRN 7/62 | |
| Luggage Brake Van | RM 10/80 | Standard Van | RM 10/70 | |
| Brake Van (ex-LCDR) | MRN 4/71 | Cattle Van | MRN 1/63 | |

| | | |
|---|---|---|
| 20 ton Brake Van | RM | 5/71 |
| 6 ton Single Bolster Timber | | |
| Wagon | RM | 5/79 |
| 10 ton high-sided Wagon | MRN | 3/65 |
| 10 ton Coal Wagon | MRN | 3/65 |
| Double Bolster Timber Wagon | RM | 2/83 |
| Coke Wagon (1851) | MRY | 11/71 |
| | | |
| *London & South Western Railway* | | |
| 7 ton Gunpowder Van | MRC | 5/72 |
| 8 ton Refrigerated Van | MRC | 7/69 |
| 10 ton Ventilated Van | MRN | 2/68 |
| 10 ton Ventilated Van (fitted) | MRN | 8/68 |
| Box Van | RM | 11/70 |
| 10 ton Brake Van | MRC | 12/64 |
| | RM | 6/71 |
| Brake Vans | RM | 7/71 |
| Ballast Brake Van | MRC | 10/64 |
| 10 ton high-sided Wagon | MRN | 7/64 |
| | MRN | 2/69 |
| 12 ton high-sided Wagon with | | |
| Bar | MRN | 4/64 |
| Stone Block Wagons | MRC | 7/65 |
| Single Bolster Wagon | MRN | 9/65 |
| Drop-side Ballast Wagons | MRC | 1/65 |
| | | |
| *South Eastern & Chatham Railway* | | |
| Van (1851) | MRY | 4/78 |
| 10 ton Ventilated Van | MRC | 5/69 |
| Brake Van (1860) | MRY | 4/78 |
| 20 ton 6 wheel Brake Van | MRC | 10/62 |
| | RM | 8/71 |

33

**SR 25 ton Bogie Brake Van**  *MRC 12/66*

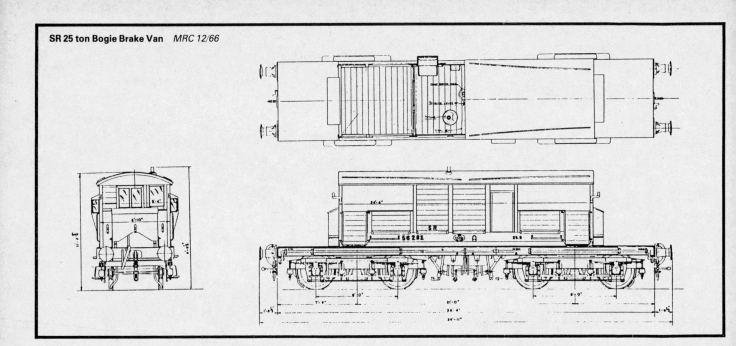

| | | |
|---|---|---|
| 25 ton Brake Van | RM | 4/71 |
| 8 ton high-sided Goods/Mineral Wagon | RM | 7/78 |
| 10 ton Open Wagon | MRC | 7/71 |
| 10 ton Open Wagon (round end) | MRN | 12/59 |
| | MRN | 7/67 |
| 10 ton high-sided Goods Wagon | RM | 8/77 |
| 10 ton Ballast Wagon | MRC | 7/72 |
| 12 ton Goods/Mineral Wagon | RM | 4/75 |
| Express Coal Wagon | MRY | 3/72 |

# Structures

*Southern Railway*

| | | |
|---|---|---|
| Wraysbury Station | MRC | 4/83 |
| Station Nameboard | MRC | 11/68 |
| | RM | 4/78 |
| | MRC | 9/84 |
| Station Valance | MRN | 2/62 |
| Platform Seats | MRC | 7/66 |
| **Signalboxes:** | | |
| Brockenhurst 'B' | RM | 1/80 |
| | RM | 3/80 |
| Fawley | RM | 10/73 |
| Goods Shed – Swanage | RM | 6/77 |
| Loading Gauge | MRC | 8/71 |
| Yard Clock | MRY | 10/71 |
| Loco Shed – Three Bridges | MRY | 3/76 |
| Shunter's WC | MRY | 9/84 |
| Huts (Concrete) | MRY | 5/72 |
| Fences | MRN | 2/67 |
| | MRC | 11/68 |
| Gradient Post | MRC | 9/84 |
| Mile Post | MRC | 9/84 |
| Notices | MRC | 11/68 |
| | RM | 2/71 |
| Siding Gate | MRY | 3/72 |
| Buffer Stops | MRY | 4/72 |
| **Signals:** | | |
| Rail Built Post | MRY | 1/81 |
| Finial | MRN | 11/62 |
| Summary | MRC | 10/83 |

*London, Brighton & South Coast Railway*

**Stations:**

| | | |
|---|---|---|
| Glynde | MRY | 4/78 |
| Purley Oaks | MRC | 11/60 |
| Rotherfield | MRN | 3/60 |
| Slinfold | RM | 4/69 |

| | | |
|---|---|---|
| Station Nameboard | RM | 7/66 |
| Station Valance | MRN | 11/60 |
| **Signalboxes:** | | |
| Crawley | MRC | 9/64 |
| Epsom | MRC | 11/65 |
| Glynde | MRY | 4/78 |
| Standard Brick Type | MRC | 1/64 |
| Standard Wood Type | MRC | 6/64 |
| | MRC | 6/82 |
| Goods Shed – Eastbourne | RM | 5/73 |
| Buffer Stops | MRY | 11/76 |
| Signal – Ground | MRC | 1/85 |
| Signals – Summary | MRC | 10/83 |

*London & South Western Railway*

**Stations:**

| | | |
|---|---|---|
| Bere Ferrers – Platform Shelter | MRC | 9/84 |
| Corfe Castle | RM | 10/76 |
| | RM | 11/76 |
| Dorchester | MRC | 11/77 |
| | MRC | 12/77 |
| | MRC | 1/78 |
| | MRC | 4/78 |
| | MRC | 5/78 |
| Moreton | MRN | 9/68 |
| | MRN | 10/68 |
| Redbridge – Platform Shelter | RM | 7/74 |
| St Margarets | MRC | 11/63 |
| Swanage | RM | 5/77 |
| Teddington | MRC | 8/60 |
| Totton | RM | 2/70 |
| Wareham – Island Platform | MRY | 3/73 |
| West Moors | MRN | 12/62 |
| | MRY | 12/72 |
| Wool | MRC | 9/73 |
| Whitchurch | MRC | 4/80 |
| Footbridge | MRY | 4/73 |
| | MRC | 10/73 |
| | RM | 1/74 |
| Station Nameboard | RM | 7/66 |
| | MRN | 9/68 |
| | RM | 4/78 |
| Station Lamps | MRC | 6/71 |
| Platform Barrows | MRC | 6/65 |
| **Signalboxes:** | | |
| Bere Ferrers | MRC | 9/84 |
| Claygate | RM | 4/68 |
| | RM | 6/69 |

| | | |
|---|---|---|
| Corfe Castle | RM | 12/76 |
| Ilfracombe | RM | 8/70 |
| Moreton | MRN | 9/68 |
| Wimborne | MRY | 2/73 |
| Wool | MRC | 9/73 |
| Worgret Jcn | RM | 4/78 |
| Ground Frame | MRC | 5/78 |
| | RM | 2/85 |
| **Goods Sheds:** | | |
| Brockenhurst | RM | 5/72 |
| Corfe Castle | RM | 1/78 |
| Dorchester | RM | 2/78 |
| | RM | 4/78 |
| Moreton | MRN | 9/68 |
| Wool | MRC | 9/73 |
| Goods Warehouse – Walton-on-Thames | MRC | 9/75 |
| Cattle pens | MRC | 2/78 |
| | MRC | 5/78 |
| Goods Office | RM | 4/78 |
| Merchants Office | RM | 7/62 |
| Yard Lamps | MRC | 9/71 |
| Loco Shed – Dorchester | MRC | 7/78 |
| Locomen's Dormitory – Dorchester | MRC | 7/78 |
| Lamp Room | MRC | 8/73 |
| | MRC | 11/77 |
| Crossing Keeper's House | MRN | 12/62 |
| | MRY | 11/72 |
| | RM | 2/78 |
| Crossing Gates | MRN | 9/68 |
| | MRC | 8/73 |
| | RM | 11/78 |
| Huts | MRN | 9/68 |
| | MRY | 10/72 |
| | MRC | 11/77 |
| Gas lamp | MRC | 9/84 |
| Road Overbridge | MRY | 2/81 |
| Water Tank | RM | 1/63 |
| | MRY | 6/73 |
| Water Tower | MRY | 3/81 |
| Loading Gauge | MRY | 8/73 |
| Buffer Stops | MRC | 9/65 |
| | RM | 6/70 |
| Gradient Post | MRN | 11/63 |
| **Signals:** | | |
| 2 Doll Bracket | MRY | 1/81 |
| Ground | MRC | 1/85 |
| Summary | MRC | 10/83 |

## South Eastern & Chatham Railway

# Track Plans

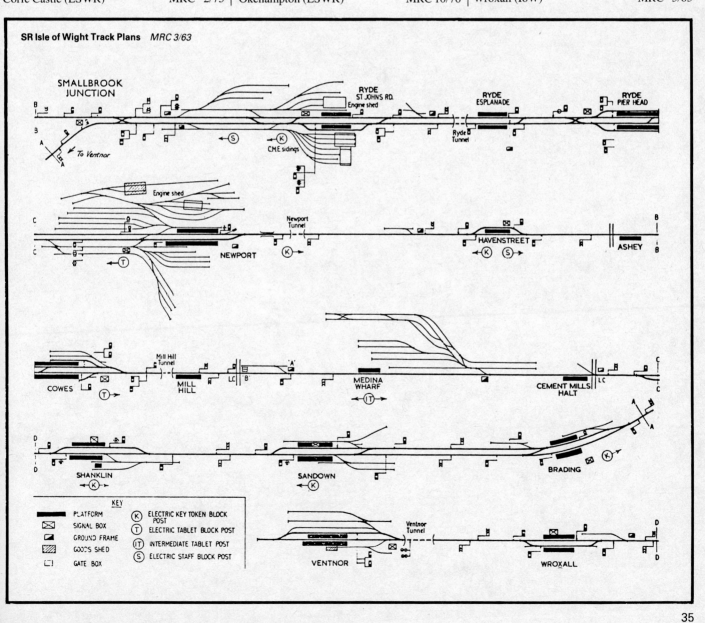

SR Isle of Wight Track Plans MRC 3/63

# Other Railways

**Belfast & County Down Railway**
Signals Summary — MRC 8/84

**Bideford, Westward Ho! & Appledore Railway**
2-4-2T — MRC 2/85
Railcar – proposed — MRC 6/85

**City & South London Railway**
Electric Loco No 10 — MRC 11/70
Coach — MRC 11/70

**Coras Iompair Eireann**
0-6-0T — MRC 5/72
Diesel Loco Class A — MRN 6/68
Diesel Loco Class B141 — MRY 3/77
12 ton Brake Van — MRY 1/77
Signal Box – Carlow — RM 3/78

**Cork, Bandon & South Coast Railway**
4-6-0T Class B4 — MRC 5/70
Station – Waterfall — MRY 6/76
Track Plan – Waterfall — MRY 6/76

**Crystal Palace Pneumatic Railway**
4 wheel Carriage — MRY 9/81
Loco Shed — MRY 9/81
Equipment — MRY 9/81

**Derwent Valley Light Railway**
Station — MRN 1/60
— MRN 2/60

**Dundalk, Newry & Greenore Railway**
6 wheel Passenger Brake Van — MRN 12/59
Signals Summary — MRC 8/84

**Easingwold Railway**
0-6-0ST No 2 – Hudswell Clarke — MRN 9/69

**East Kent Railway**
4-4-2T No 5 — MRN 6/71
0-6-0T No 4 (SR No 948) — RM 9/66

**Glasgow Corporation**
Subway Car — MRC 5/77

**Great Northern Railway (Ireland)**
Signals Summary — MRC 8/84

**Great Southern & Western Railway**
4-6-0 Class 800 — MRY 10/77
4-4-0 Class D19 — MRY 2/76
— MRY 8/80
10 ton Open Wagon — MRY 8/76
Signals Summary — MRC 8/84

**Kent & East Sussex Railway**
2-4-0T *Northian* — MRN 12/68
2-4-0T *Tenterden* — MRN 1/69
0-6-0ST No 4 — MRN 6/70
0-6-0ST No 8 *Hesperus* — MRN 2/70
0-8-0T *Hecate* — MRN 12/69
Pickering Steam Railcar — MRN 3/70
4 wheel Third Coach — MRN 2/69

4 wheel Brake Third Coach
  (ex-LSWR) — MRN 12/69
4 wheel Brake Van (ex-NLR) — MRN 1/71
Pickering Stock — MRN 1/70
Open Wagon — MRN 3/69
Brake Van — MRN 3/69
Station – Rolvenden — MRN 4/69
Station – Tenterden — MRN 8/69
Goods Shed – Tenterden — RM 10/72
Loco Shed – Rolvenden — MRN 5/69
Hut — MRN 4/69
Track Plan – Rolvenden — RM 5/63
— MRN 4/69
Track Plan – Tenterden — MRN 8/69

**Hellingly Hospital Railway**
Electric Loco — MRN 9/60

**Liverpool Overhead Railway**
40' Motor Second Coach — MRC 6/83
45' Motor Second Coach — MRC 6/83
Trailer First — MRC 6/83
Signal Finial — MRN 9/62
— MRN 10/62

**London Transport**
0-6-0T No L30 — MRN 4/68
Motor Car (1927) — MRN 3/62
Control Car (1927) — MRN 4/63
C69 Stock — RM 1/71
Victoria Line Stock — RM 5/68
1973 Stock — RM 10/78

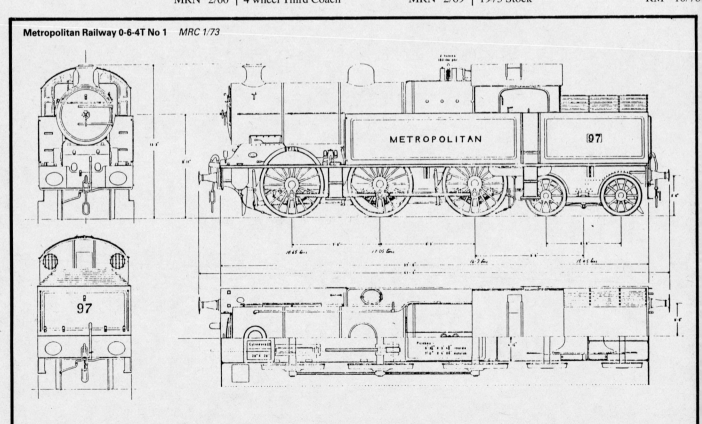

**Metropolitan Railway 0-6-4T No 1**  *MRC 1/73*

*Above left:* **Liverpool Overhead Railway standard three-car train with motor coach No 3 leading. (Drawing MRC 6/83).** *C. E. Box*

*Left:* **Metropolitan Railway 4-4-0T No 27 fitted with condensing equipment. (Drawing RM 2/67).**
*London Transport*

# Narrow Gauge Railways

**Ashover Light Railway**
4-6-0T Baldwin — MRC 2/83

**Castlederg & Victoria Bridge Tramway**
2-6-0T — RM 5/85

**Cavan & Leitrim Railway**
Brake Van — MRY 12/71
5 ton Open Wagon — MRY 12/71
6 ton Open Wagon — MRY 12/71

**Cork & Muskerry Railway**
4-4-0T — RM 2/85

**County Donegal Railway**
4-6-0T — MRN 7/63
2-6-4T Class 5a — RM 12/84
Railbus No 7 — MRC 7/61
36′ Composite Coach — MRY 2/79
Van — MRY 5/73
— MRY 6/73
Goods/Cattle Van — MRY 6/73
Open Wagon — MRY 5/73
— MRY 6/73

**Dinorwic Slate Quarries**
0-4-0T Avonside (1933) — MRY 3/73

**Festiniog Railway**
4 wheel First Coach — MRN 10/66
First Coach (1965) — MRN 10/66
36′ Coach – Aluminium Body — MRY 1/73
Minffordd station — RM 1/75

**Glyn Valley Tramway**
0-4-2T Beyer Peacock — MRN 6/67
4-6-0T Baldwin No 4 (original
  condition) — MRC 2/83

**Isle of Man Railway**
2-4-0T Nos 1-3 — MRY 3/73
2-4-0T Nos 4-6 — MRY 4/74
2-4-0T Nos 7-9 — MRY 5/74
2-4-0T Nos 10-13 — MRY 6/74
2-4-0T No 16 Mannin — MRN 2/63
2-4-0T No 1 Sutherland — RM 9/83
2-4-0T No 4 Loch — MRN 2/60
Brake Coach — MRN 2/60
Station – Kirk Braddon — MRC 2/73
Station – Peal — RM 4/74
Goods Shed – Kirk Michael — RM 11/67
Track Plan – Foxdale — RM 9/83
Signals — MRN 10/69

**Letterkenny & Burtonport Railway**
4-6-0T Andrew Barclay — MRN 5/62

**Londonderry & Lough Swilly Railway**
4-8-4T — RM 12/84

**Lynton & Barnstaple Railway**
2-6-2T Manning Wardle — MRC 4/84
Third Coaches — MRC 9/83

**Northern Counties Committee**
2-4-2T Class S — MRN 8/65

Saloon Coach — MRN 12/64

**Padarn Railway**
0-6-0T — MRY 5/73

**Penrhyn Quarry Railway**
0-4-0T Avonside (1933) — MRY 3/73
0-4-0ST Linda – Hunslet (1893) — MRY 10/76
0-4-0ST Charles – Hunslet
  (1907) — MRY 3/78

**Pentewan Railway**
Hopper Wagon — MRN 2/69
Track Plan – Pentewan — MRN 2/69

**Schull & Skibbereen Railway**
4-4-0T — MRN 7/69
First Coach — MRC 10/68
Third Coach — MRC 10/68
Track Plan – Schull — MRN 6/69

**Snailbeach District Railway**
4-6-0T Nos 3 & 4 – Baldwin — MRC 2/83
Track Plan – Snailbeach Jcn — RM 9/80

**Southwold Railway**
2-4-2T No 1 Southwold — MRN 11/63
— MRC 1/79

2-4-0T No 3 Blyth (rebuilt) — MRC 1/79
0-6-2T No 4 Wenhaston — MRC 1/79
Coaches — MRC 2/79
Wagons — MRC 4/79
**Stations and Track Plans:**
  Blythburgh — MRC 6/79
  Halesworth — MRC 6/79
  Southwold — MRC 5/79
  Walberswick — MRC 6/79
  Wenhaston — MRC 6/79

**Swanage Tramway**
Track Plan — MRY 4/78

**Talyllyn Railway**
0-4-2ST No 1 Talyllyn — MRN 9/65
0-4-0WT No 2 Dolgoch — MRN 10/65
0-4-2ST No 4 Edward Thomas — RM 11/65
4 wheel Coaches — MRN 9/65
Third Coach — MRN 6/65
4 wheel Brake Coach — MRN 9/65
Wagon — MRN 9/65
Station – Abergynolwyn — RM 8/75

**Tralee & Dingle Railway**
2-6-0T No 2 (Hunslet) — RM 2/77
2-6-2T No 5 (Hunslet) — RM 5/62
Composite Coach — MRN 7/63
Full Brake — MRN 7/63

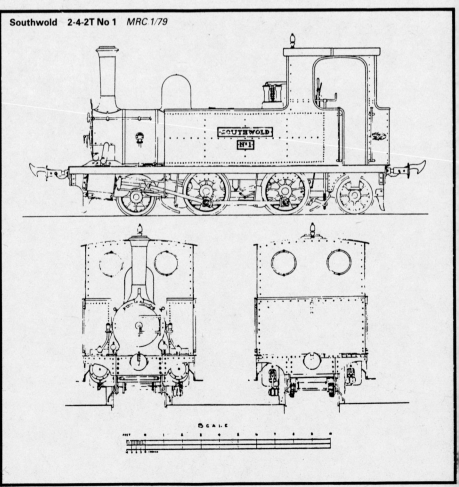

**Southwold 2-4-2T No 1**  *MRC 1/79*

| Welsh Highland Railway | | |
|---|---|---|
| 4-6-0T No 590 (Baldwin) | MRC | 2/83 |
| Composite Coach | MRN | 7/63 |
| Brake Coach | MRN | 7/63 |

| Welshpool & Llanfair Railway | | |
|---|---|---|
| 2-6-2T No 14 (ex-Sierra Leone Rly) | MRY | 1/76 |
| Open Wagon | MRC | 2/65 |

| West Clare Railway | | |
|---|---|---|
| Diesel – Walker Bros | MRY | 12/74 |
| | RM | 6/85 |
| Horse Box | MRY | 2/72 |
| Van | MRY | 1/72 |
| Open Wagon | MRY | 1/72 |
| Flat Wagon | MRY | 1/72 |
| Cattle Truck | MRY | 1/72 |

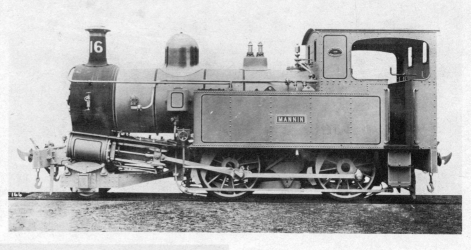

**Above:** Isle of Man Railway 2-4-0T No 16 *Mannin*, built Beyer Peacock 1926. (Drawing MRN 2/63). *Ian Allan Library*

**Left:** Talyllyn Railway 0-4-0WT No 2 *Dolgoch* and 0-4-2ST No 1 *Talyllyn* in a posed view at Pendre with a train of the railway's four wheel coaches. (Drawings MRN 9/65 and 10/65). *Locomotive Publishing Co (5655)*

**Below:** Padarn Railway 4ft gauge 0-6-0T *Dinorwic*, built Hunslet 1882, seen at Llanberis. (Drawing MRY 5/73). *R. E. Vincent*

# Industrial Locomotives

| | |
|---|---|
| **Armstrong – Whitworth** | |
| 880hp Diesel (1933) | MRY 6/77 |
| | |
| *The Lady Armstrong* | |
| Diesel (1932) | MRY 3/85 |
| | |
| *Avonside* | |
| 0-6-0ST Class B3 | RM 10/75 |
| 0-4-0ST Class SS | RM 11/74 |
| 0-4-0T 2'0" Gauge (1933) | MRY 3/73 |
| | |
| *Baldwin Loco Works* | |
| 4-6-0T 60cm Gauge | MRC 2/83 |
| | |
| *Andrew Barclay* | |
| 0-4-0T Class E | MRN 2/67 |
| 0-4-0T | RM 12/74 |
| | |
| *Beyer Peacock* | |
| 0-4-0 + 0-4-0T Garratt | RM 11/72 |
| | |
| *Brush* | |
| 300hp Diesel | MRC 11/59 |
| | |
| *Fowler* | |
| 176hp Diesel | MRC 11/59 |
| | |
| *Hawthorn Leslie* | |
| 0-4-0ST *Invincible* | RM 5/67 |
| | |
| *Hundswell Clarke* | |
| 252hp Diesel | MRY 3/84 |
| | |
| *Hunslet Engine Company* | |
| 4-6-0T 60cm Gauge (1916) | MRY 4/76 |
| | MRY 7/76 |
| | MRY 8/76 |
| 0-6-0ST 16" *Robert Nelson No 4* | RM 9/72 |
| 0-6-0ST *Belvoir* – 3' Gauge | MRN 4/68 |
| 0-4-0T Cadbury No 9 | RM 11/65 |
| 0-4-0ST Bass (Rebuilt) | RM 4/72 |
| 0-4-0T | MRN 9/66 |
| | MRN 3/67 |

| | |
|---|---|
| 0-4-0ST Quarry | MRN 9/66 |
| | MRN 11/66 |
| | MRN 3/67 |
| 325hp Diesel | MRC 10/72 |
| | |
| *Inglis* | |
| 0-4-0ST | RM 3/69 |
| | |
| *Kerr Stewart* | |
| 0-6-0T 'Victory' Class | RM 9/66 |
| Diesel No 4421 (1929) | RM 5/79 |
| 30hp Std NG Diesel | MRC 11/77 |
| 60hp Std NG Diesel | MRC 11/77 |
| 90hp Std NG Diesel | MRC 11/77 |
| | |
| *Kitson* | |
| 0-6-0ST Class A | RM 9/74 |
| | |
| *Lister Blackstone* | |
| Diesel Type RM3 | RM 10/78 |
| | |
| *Manning Wardle* | |
| 0-6-0ST Class M | RM 4/74 |
| | RM 8/74 |
| 0-6-0ST 18" *Littleton No 4/No 5* | RM 5/70 |
| 0-6-0ST *Corston* (1890) | MRN 8/68 |
| 0-6-0ST Old Class 1 (1859) | RM 7/74 |
| 0-6-0ST Long Boiler | |
| The Welshman | RM 10/70 |
| 0-8-0T | RM 6/76 |
| 0-4-0ST Class B | RM 1/74 |
| 0-4-0ST Class C | RM 1/74 |
| 0-4-0ST *Rosalind* (1874) | RM 12/75 |
| 0-6-0 *Pentewan* 2'6" Gauge | MRY 7/77 |
| | |
| *Motor Rail* | |
| Diesel Series G | RM 1/76 |
| Diesel Series U | RM 1/76 |
| Diesel Series T | RM 1/76 |
| 48bhp Type 40S – Narrow | |
| Gauge | RM 6/75 |
| 70bhp Type 60S – Narrow | |
| Gauge | RM 6/75 |

| | |
|---|---|
| 28bhp – Narrow Gauge | RM 6/75 |
| *Neilson* | |
| 0-4-0 Single Cylinder | MRY 12/81 |
| 0-4-0ST 'Box' Tank | MRY 6/78 |
| | MRY 11/78 |
| | |
| *North British* | |
| 100hp Mine Diesel – 2'6"/3'6" | |
| Gauge | MRY 1/75 |
| | |
| *Peckett* | |
| 0-4-0ST (1929) | MRC 9/67 |
| 0-4-0ST Barrow Steelworks | RM 11/67 |
| 0-4-0ST | MRC 3/68 |
| 0-4-0FT Fireless | RM 4/66 |
| 0-6-0ST *Scaldwell* – 3' Gauge | MRN 2/66 |
| | |
| *Robert Stephenson & Hawthorn* | |
| 0-4-0ST 14" | RM 4/67 |
| 0-4-0CT Crane Tank | RM 10/71 |
| | |
| *Ruston Hornsby* | |
| Diesel Type 48DS | RM 5/73 |
| 200hp Diesel | MRC 11/59 |
| 16/20hp Diesel – 2' Gauge | MRN 8/61 |
| | RM 4/75 |
| 44/48hp Diesel – 2' Gauge | RM 4/75 |
| | |
| *Sentinel* | |
| Diesel-hydraulic | RM 6/68 |
| | |
| *Yorkshire Engine Company* | |
| 0-4-0ST United Steel Co | |
| (1934-1949) | RM 2/79 |
| | |
| *Miscellaneous* | |
| 0-4-0 *Puffing Billy* | MRY 1/79 |
| Lartigue Vertical Boiler | MRY 1/77 |
| 0-4-0 Boulton 'Liliputan' – 2' | |
| Gauge (1863) | MRY 1/82 |

*Above:* **Guest, Keen Baldwins Iron & Steel Co 0-4-0 + 0-4-0T Beyer Garratt No 12 for East Moors Works Cardiff, built Beyer Peacock (6779/1934). (Drawing RM 11/72).** *Locomotive Publishing Co (9018)*

*Above:* **Doxford Shipyard 0-4-0CT,** *Hendon,* **built Robert Stephenson & Hawthorn (7007/1940). (Drawing RM 10/71).** *R. W. Courtney*

*Left:* **Hawthorn Leslie 0-4-0ST** *Invincible* **(3135/1915) in action at RAE Farnborough. (Drawing RM 5/67).** *Ministry of Defence*

*Below :* **Prototype Fowler 176hp 0-4-0 diesel-mechanical shunter in works grey livery on test at Middleton. (Drawing MRC 11/59).** *Ian Allan Library*

# Road Vehicles

| | |
|---|---|
| **Albion** | |
| 5 ton Parcel Van – LMSR | MRC 4/67 |
| | |
| **AEC** | |
| Renown Double Deck Bus | MRC 3/76 |
| Majesty 6 ton Lorry | MRC 6/78 |
| Mandator Tractive Unit and Trailer | MRC 2/71 |
| Mammoth Major Mk 1 Lorry | MRC 12/78 |
| | |
| **Bedford** | |
| OWB Single Deck Bus | MRC 9/79 |
| OB Bus | MRC 12/72 |
| YRT/Caetano Coach | MRC 12/79 |
| OSB Tipper Lorry | MRC 9/83 |
| 3 ton Van | MRC 11/66 |
| 8 cwt Van – Model HAV | MRC 12/75 |
| | |
| **Bristol** | |
| K Double deck Bus | MRC 10/70 |
| Lodekka Bus | MRN 7/67 |
| VRT/SL (ECW Body) Bus | MRC 10/74 |
| L6B Royal Blue Coach | MRC 3/73 |
| LL6B Western National Coach | MRC 3/81 |
| RELH/ECW Coach | MRC 12/73 |
| | |
| **BMMO** | |
| Type D1 (AD2) Double deck Bus | MRC 3/75 |
| Type C3 Coach | MRC 12/79 |
| | |
| **Chevrolet** | |
| LQ Coach (1929) | MRC 6/78 |
| | |
| **Crossley** | |
| DD42 Bus | MRC 9/72 |
| | |
| **Daimler** | |
| Y Type Double deck Bus (1916) | MRC 6/77 |
| Roadliner Single deck Bus | MRC 3/67 |
| CVD6 Bus | MRC 9/73 |
| Lorry – LYR (1911) | MRC 11/68 |
| | |
| **Dennis** | |
| Parcel Van (1931) | MRC 3/70 |
| 2 ton Parcel Van – LMSR | MRC 1/68 |
| 2 ton Platform Lorry – LMSR | MRC 8/68 |
| 10 ton Tipper Lorry – LMSR | MRC 4/68 |

| | |
|---|---|
| **ERF** | |
| Road Tanker | MRC 11/70 |
| | |
| **Foden** | |
| FE/FG Trucks | MRC 3/76 |
| Type C 6 ton Steam Wagon | MRC 12/78 |
| | MRC 6/79 |
| | |
| **Ford** | |
| 3 ton Chassis D300 | MRC 11/66 |
| | |
| **Horsedrawn** | |
| FR Parcels Van | MRY 10/76 |
| GCR Parcels Van | MRY 1/85 |
| LYR Van | MRY 1/83 |
| LNWR Lorry | MRY 10/76 |
| LNWR Van | MRY 9/83 |
| MR Trolley | MRY 9/76 |
| MR Wagon | MRY 8/83 |
| SECR Omnibus Type U | MRC 6/74 |
| | |
| **Huddersfield Corp** | |
| Tram | MRC 3/81 |
| | |
| **Karrier** | |
| 1½ ton Delivery Van – LMSR | MRC 1/68 |
| 5 ton Delivery Lorry – LMSR | MRC 6/67 |
| 10 ton Tractor LMSR | MRC 12/69 |
| | |
| **Latil** | |
| Tractor and Road-Rail Tank | MRC 9/76 |
| | |
| **Leyland** | |
| Atlantean (Liverpool Style) Double Deck Bus | MRC 9/77 |
| Titan Double Deck Bus | MRC 3/69 |
| Titan TD4C Double Deck Bus | MRC 3/77 |
| Lion PLSC3 Bus | MRC 6/68 |
| Tiger TS7, Harrington Body | MRC 7/80 |
| Ambassador Coach – Leyland/Duple | MRC 3/83 |
| Hippo Lorry | MRC 6/73 |
| Octopus Lorry | MRN 7/67 |
| Clydesdale Milk Tanker | MRC 9/79 |
| | |
| **London Transport** | |
| S Type Single Deck Bus | MRC 6/73 |
| RF Type Double Deck Bus | MRC 5/71 |
| NS Type Double Deck Bus | MRC 6/76 |

| | |
|---|---|
| | MRC 12/76 |
| Class B1/B2 Trolley Bus | MRC 6/75 |
| Class C1 Trolley Bus | MRC 6/75 |
| **Trams:** | |
| Class A | MRC 12/76 |
| Class E/1 | MRN 10/67 |
| Class E1 | MRC 12/74 |
| Class E1/R | MRC 5/69 |
| Class K | MRN 2/71 |
| Feltham | MRN 7/62 |
| | MRC 9/66 |
| | MRC 8/81 |
| Palace | MRN 5/62 |
| Merryweather Steam Tram (1890) | MRC 12/73 |
| | |
| **Metro-Scania** | |
| Single Deck Bus | MRC 12/75 |
| | |
| **Milnes-Daimler** | |
| Double Deck Bus (1905) | MRC 12/78 |
| | |
| **Morris** | |
| FJK140 – 7 ton | MRC 8/66 |
| | |
| **Portrush & Giant's Causeway** | |
| Tram | MRN 4/59 |
| | |
| **Preston** | |
| Tram | MRC 12/67 |
| | |
| **Sheffield Corp** | |
| Class 500 Tram | MRN 2/62 |
| | |
| **Scammell** | |
| 12 ton Rigid 6 Truck | MRC 12/72 |
| Routeman 11, Rigid 8 Truck | MRC 9/77 |
| Contractor Truck | MRC 3/78 |
| Trucker 11 Tanker | MRC 3/73 |
| Mechanical Horse | MRN 7/67 |
| Road/Rail Tank | MRC 9/76 |
| | |
| **Thornycroft** | |
| 1½ ton Van GWR | MRY 12/73 |
| | |
| **Vulcan** | |
| 6PF Lorry | MRC 6/78 |

*Above left:* **Royal Blue LL6B Bristol coach No 1252, LTA 731. (Drawing MRC 3/81).**

*Left:* **Sheffield tramcar No 521. (Drawing MRN 2/62).** *V. C. Jones*

*Below:* **AEC Mammoth Major petrol tanker. (Drawing MRC 12/78).** *ACV Sales Ltd*

# Industrial & Residential Structures

| | | | | | |
|---|---|---|---|---|---|
| Airfield | RM 1/84 | Harbour Master's Office – | | Mill – East Anglia | MRY 7/84 |
| Almshouse | MRC 12/81 | Weymouth | RM 5/63 | Oast House | MRY 11/83 |
| Ballast Tip | MRN 9/71 | Hotel – Eastbourne | RM 2/73 | Office/Shop Building | RM 5/76 |
| Barn | RM 1/78 | Hotel – Thame | MRC 12/80 | Oil Depot | RM 3/64 |
| | MRC 5/81 | | | | MRY 6/79 |
| Bridge | MRC 9/79 | **Houses:** | | Pub | MRC 9/69 |
| | RM 1/82 | Georgian (19th Century) | MRN 12/64 | Pylon – Grid | RM 6/70 |
| Builder's Yard | RM 2/80 | 'Georgian' (1962) | RM 1/62 | Shop | MRC 5/81 |
| Cafe | RM 7/77 | Modern | RM 1/72 | | MRC 2/83 |
| Campsite | RM 2/84 | | MRY 10/81 | Shops – Pair | MRN 3/70 |
| Church | RM 5/83 | Old | RM 8/71 | Shops – Row | MRN 12/69 |
| Colliery | RM 2/84 | | RM 9/71 | | RM 12/72 |
| Cottage | RM 7/75 | | RM 11/71 | Shop – Victorian | MRC 9/84 |
| | MRC 2/76 | | RM 12/71 | Staiths | MRN 10/66 |
| | MRY 10/76 | Regency | MRN 6/68 | | RM 2/78 |
| Cottage – Chipping Campden | MRN 3/63 | Tenement | RM 7/78 | Storage Sheds | RM 10/71 |
| Cottage – Somerset | RM 1/72 | Terrace | MRN 12/63 | Street Lamps | RM 9/77 |
| Cottage – Sussex | RM 8/69 | | RM 12/71 | Timber Storage Shed | RM 6/75 |
| Cottage – Thatched | RM 7/83 | | RM 1/72 | Timber Yard | MRY 1/79 |
| Customs House – Exeter | RM 12/81 | Town (19th Century) | MRC 8/75 | Tippler (Truck) | RM 1/77 |
| Distillery | RM 12/66 | Industrial Buildings | RM 7/77 | Tippler (Wagon) | MRY 8/79 |
| Electricity Building | RM 9/71 | Inn – Devon | RM 8/80 | Village Features | MRY 1/77 |
| Factory | RM 5/75 | Inn – Exeter | MRY 3/84 | Warehouse | RM 10/71 |
| | RM 1/76 | Lime Works | MRY 10/78 | | RM 6/75 |
| Factory – Derelict | RM 9/77 | Maltings | MRY 8/81 | | RM 7/76 |
| Forge | RM 7/75 | | MRY 6/84 | | MRC 10/82 |
| Gas Works | RM 9/60 | Merchant's Office | RM 7/62 | Windmills | RM 1/85 |
| | RM 6/61 | Mill – Farnham | MRC 7/73 | Workshop/Garage | MRC 6/83 |

44

Far left: **Two 90 ton cement storage silos at West Kilbride station. Portable diesel compressor in foreground for discharging cement from railway wagons to silo.**
British Railways (Scottish Region)

Above left: **Clapboard construction timber warehouse. (Warehouse drawings RM 10/71, 6/75, 7/76, MRC 10/82).**

Above: **Clapboard construction post windmill. (Windmill drawings RM 1/85).**

Left: **Norwich Coal Concentration Depot with 21 ton hopper wagons passing over the discharge unit.** British Rail

# Appendix

A list of books containing a significant number of locomotive, rolling stock or structure drawings is presented below. The reader should be aware that many other books, particularly those dealing with specific railway companies, frequently contain relevant drawings.

Abbreviations used for the publishers of books listed in this appendix are as follows:

IA       Ian Allan Ltd
BB       Bradford Barton
DC       David and Charles
HMRS     Historical Model Railway Society
OKP      Oakwood Press
OPC      Oxford Publishing Company
WSP      Wild Swan Publications

## British Railways

*BR Motive Power Since 1948*, B. Cooper (IA)
*BR Standard Steam Locomotives to Scale*, I. Beattie (BB)
*A Pictorial Record of British Railways Standard Steam Locomotives*, E. Talbot (OPC)
*BR Main Line Diesels in 4mm Scale*, R. S. Carter (IA)
*BR Electric Locomotives in 4mm Scale*, R. S. Carter (IA)
*British Rail Fleet Survey Vol 1: Early Prototype and Pilot Scheme Diesel-Electrics*, B. Haresnape (IA)
*British Rail Fleet Survey Vol 2: Western Region Diesel-Hydraulics*, B. Haresnape (IA)
*British Rail Fleet Survey Vol 3: Production Diesel-Electrics Types 4 and 5*, B. Haresnape (IA)
*British Rail Fleet Survey Vol 4: Production Diesel-Electrics Types 1-3*, B. Haresnape (IA)
*British Rail Fleet Survey Vol 5: High Speed Trains*, B. Haresnape (IA)
*British Rail Fleet Survey Vol 6: Electric Locomotives*, B. Haresnape (IA)
*British Rail Fleet Survey Vol 7: Diesel Shunters*, B. Haresnape (IA)
*British Rail Fleet Survey Vol 8: Diesel Multiple-Units – The First Generation*, B. Haresnape (IA)
*A Pictorial Record of the Diesel Shunter*, C. Marsden (OPC)

## Great Western Railway

*A Pictorial Record of Great Western Engines*, J. H. Russell (OPC)
*A Pictorial Record of Great Western Absorbed Engines*, J. H. Russell (OPC)
*GWR Locomotives to Scale*, I. Beattie (BB)
*A Pictorial Record of Great Western Coaches Part 1: 1838-1913*, J. H. Russell (OPC)
*A Pictorial Record of Great Western Coaches Part 2: 1903-1948*, J. H. Russell (OPC)
*Great Western Coaches Appendix Vol. 1: Standard Passenger Stock*, J. H. Russell (OPC)

*Great Western Coaches Appendix Vol. 2: Special Duty Coaches and the Brown Vehicles*, J. H. Russell (OPC)
*A Pictorial Record of Great Western Wagons*, J. H. Russell (OPC)
*Great Western Wagons Appendix*, J. H. Russell (OPC)
*Great Western Wagons Plan Book*, J. H. Russell (OPC)
*A History of GWR Goods Wagons Vols 1 and 2*, A. G. Atkins et al. (DC)
*All About GWR Iron Minks*, J. H. Lewis et al. (HMRS)
*An Historical Survey of Selected Great Western Stations*, R. Clark (OPC).
*An Historical Survey of Selected Great Western Stations Vol 2*, R. Clark (OPC)
*An Historical Survey of Selected Great Western Stations Vol 3*. R. Clark (OPC)
*A Pictorial Record of Great Western Architecture*, A. Vaughan (OPC)
*Great Western Branch Line Termini*, P. Karau (OPC)
*GWR Country Stations*, C. Leigh (IA)
*GWR Country Stations Vol 2*, C. Leigh (IA)
*An Historical Survey of Great Western Engine Sheds – 1947*, E. Lyons (OPC)
*An Historical Survey of Great Western Engine Sheds 1837-1947*, E. Lyons and E. Mountford (OPC)
*A Pictorial Record of Great Western Signalling*, A. Vaughan (OPC)
*Historical Survey of the Forest of Dean Railways*, P. Smith (OPC)
*The Cowbridge Railway*, C. Chapman (OPC)
*The Didcot, Newbury and Southampton Railway*, P. Karau et al. (OPC)
*Princes Risborough – Thame – Oxford Railway*, R. Lingard (OPC)

## London, Midland & Scottish Railway

*LMSR Locomotives to Scale*, I. Beattie (BB)
*A History of Highland Locomotives*, P. Tatlow (OPC)
*North Staffordshire Railway Locomotives and Rolling Stock*, R. W. Rush (OKP)
*Historic Carriage Drawings in 4mm Scale Vol 1*, D. Jenkinson and N. Campling (IA)
*The LMS Coach 1923-1957*, R. Essery and D. Jenkinson (IA)
*An Illustrated History of LMS Coaches*, D. Jenkinson and R. Essery (OPC)
*A Register of West Coast Joint Stock*, R. Casserley and P. Millard (HMRS)
*An Illustrated History of LNWR Coaches*, D. Jenkinson (OPC)
*Midland Carriages*, D. Jenkinson and R. Essery (OPC)
*Midland Railway Carriages Vol 1*, R. Lacy and G. Dow (WSP)
*Lancashire & Yorkshire Passenger Stock*, R. W. Rush (OKP)
*The LMS Wagon*, R. J. Essery and K. R. Morgan (DC)
*An Illustrated History of LMS Wagons Vol 1*,

R. J. Essery (OPC)
*An Illustrated History of LMS Wagons Vol 2*, R. J. Essery (OPC)
*An Illustrated History of Midland Wagons Vol 1*, R. J. Essery (OPC)
*An Illustrated History of Midland Wagons Vol 2*, R. J. Essery (OPC)
*An Historical Survey of Selected LMS Stations Vol 1*, R. Preston Hendry and R. Powell Hendry (OPC)
*An Historical Survey of the Chester to Holyhead Railway*, R. Anderson and G. Fox (OPC)
*A Pictorial Record of LMS Architecture*, R. Anderson and G. Fox (OPC)
*Rails in the Fells* (Settle & Carlisle), D. Jenkinson (PECO)
*LMS Engine Sheds Vol 1 (LNWR)*, C. Hawkins and G. Reeve (WSP)
*LMS Engine Sheds Vol 2 (MR)*, C. Hawkins and G. Reeve (WSP)
*LMS Engine Sheds Vol 3 (LYR)*, C. Hawkins and G. Reeve (WSP)
*LMS Engine Sheds Vol 4 (FR, LTS, SDJR, SMJR)*, C. Hawkins and G. Reeve (WSP)
*A Pictorial Record of LNWR Signalling*, R. D. Foster (OPC)

## London & North Eastern Railway

*LNER Locomotives to Scale*, I. Beattie (BB)
*East Coast Pacifics at Work*, P. N. Townend (IA)
*Great Eastern Railway 0-4-4T*, G. Pember (GER Society)
*Great Central Vols 1-3*, G. Dow (IA)
*Album of North Eastern Railway Drawings*, Anon (NER Association)
*Historic Carriage Drawings in 4mm Scale Vol 1*, D. Jenkinson and N. Campling (IA)
*A Pictorial History of LNER Wagons*, P. Tatlow (OPC)
*A Pictorial Record of LNER Constituent Signalling*, A. MacLean (OPC)

## Southern Railway

*Southern Locomotives to Scale*, I. Beattie (BB)
*The Maunsell Moguls*, J. W. P. Rowledge (OKP)
*The Locomotives of the London, Brighton & South Coast Railway*, F. Burtt (Harvester Press)
*Bulleid Coaches in 4mm Scale*, S. W. Stevens-Stratten (IA)
*Carriage Stock of the LBSCR*, P. J. Newbury (OKP)
*Illustrated History of Southern Wagons Vol 1: LSWR and SDJR*, G. Bixley et al. (OPC)
*An Historical Survey of Selected Southern Stations*, G. Pryer and G. Bowring (OPC)
*Southern Country Stations: London & South Western Railway*, R. Antell (IA)
*Southern Country Stations: South Eastern & Chatham Railway*, J. Minnis (IA)

Branch Lines of the Southern Railway, G.
Reeve and C. Hawkins (WSP)

An Historical Survey of Southern Sheds
1923-1947, C. Hawkins and G. Reeve (OPC)

A Pictorial Record of Southern Signals, G.
Pryer (OPC)

Period Railway Modelling: Buildings, V.
Thompson (PECO)

## Various

Historic Locomotive Drawings in 4mm Scale,
F. J. Roche (IA)

Nineteenth Century Railway Drawings in
4mm Scale, A. Prior (DC)

Locomotives Worth Modelling, F. C.
Hambleton (Argus)

British Steam Railcars, R. W. Rush (OKP)

The Festiniog Railway Vol 2: Locomotives
and Rolling Stock, J. I. C. Boyd (OKP)

Portrait of the Lynton and Barnstaple Railway,
C. Leigh (IA)

British Goods Wagons from 1887 to the
Present Day, R. J. Essery et al. (DC)

Historic Wagon Drawings in 4mm Scale, F. J.
Roche (IA)

Petroleum Rail Tank Wagons of Britain, R.
Tourret (author)

British Electric Tramcar Designs 1885-1950,
R. W. Rush (OPC)

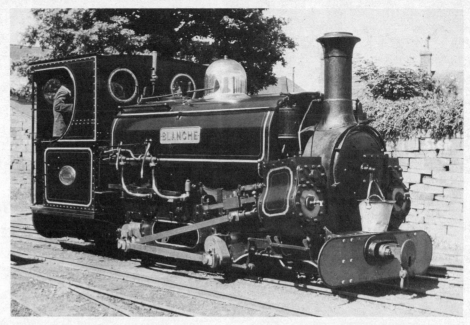

*Above:* **Penrhyn Railway 0-4-0ST *Blanche* at Bethesda, built Hunslet (589/1893). (Drawing MRY 10/76).** *R. E. Vincent*

*Below:* **British Railways, Western Region, Yatton** station on 4 April 1963. Swindon Type 4 'Warship' No D802 *Sir Brian Robertson* on 9.45am Paddington–Weston-super-Mare. Ivatt '2MT' 2-6-2T No 41248 on 2.00pm Yatton–Witham. (Track plan of Yatton RM 12/59. 'Warship' B-B drawing MRC 10/70). *Leslie Sandler*

*Above:* LMS 'Royal Scot' class 4-6-0 No 6139 *Ajax* in original condition passes Bushey station. (Drawing RM 11/60).  *Ian Allan Library*

*Left:* 4-REP electric multiple-unit No 3003 for the Southern Region Bournemouth electrification passes Micheldever on a training run on 18 March 1967 when new. (Drawings MRC 7/67).
*John H. Bird*

*Below:* Kent and East Sussex Railway 2-4-0T *Tenterden* at Rolvenden, built Hawthorn Leslie (2420/1899). (Drawing MRN 1/69).
*Ian Allan Library*